Principles for Successful Living

10 principles every person must know to live victoriously

Terry Tripp

Principles For Successful Living
Published by Terry Tripp Ministries Publications

Cover design by Tony Young of His Image Design
Edited by Mary Sloan for Productive Rhythm

Printed in the United States of America
www.instantpublisher.com

Published by: Terry Tripp Ministries Publications
P.O. Box 899
Gallatin, TN 37066
www.terrytripp.com

Acknowledgements

My Lord and Savior, Jesus Christ; He is the description of how to walk victoriously and successfully in life.

My Wife, Kim; You are the Proverbs 31 woman. Our marriage is favored because you are a good wife (Proverbs 18:22). Your love and strength have helped me be the man I am today. I call you blessed!

My Grandfathers, Elvin Tripp and Clayton Rhodes; These two men made a quality decision to place God's Word as the most important asset in their life. Today, I am living out the success of their decision.

My Dad, Laverne Tripp; Only eternity will tell of the wisdom you've deposited in my life. You've shown me that success is growth... one day at a time. Success is also a good name; you've given me that as well. I am forever grateful.

My Brother, Pastor Robb Tripp; When everything in the natural screamed, "Don't do it." You & Shanda held on to the vision... that's success!

My Father-in-law, Joel Sloan; Your "Never give up" attitude has been a great inspiration to me. You are a blessing to my life!

The Passionate Society; You are the greatest partners a ministry could ever have. Kim and I could not do all we are doing without you. Stay Passionate about the Word.

To others who have imparted the success of God's Word into my life: Pastor Charles Cowan and Faith is The Victory Bible College (Brian Cowan, Margaret Bomar, Phil Scott), Kenneth & Gloria Copeland, Mylon & Christi Le Fevre, James Payne, Darlene Bishop, Alick, Stephanie and Dean Clark, Pastor Carl & Brenda Morris, Pastor Donnie McClurkin, Pastor Joseph Morgan, Dr. Ron Cottle, Charles Capps, Pastor Ron and Hope Carpenter, Dr. Creflo Dollar, Bishop Henry Fernandez, Michelle McKinney Hammond, Jerry Savelle, Jesse and Sybil Evatte, Jesse Duplantis, Joyce Meyer, Barney and Gail Blackwell, Pastor Joel Osteen, Bishop Jon Scott, Robin Bullock, Kenneth Hagin, Pastor Happy and Jeanne Caldwell, Roger and Lynn Neal, Buster Wilmore, Keith Moore.

I would like to thank Tony Young, founder of His Image Design, for the layout and design of all my books and CDs. You're a gifted man and a blessing to this ministry.

Chapters

Preface

The Word of God (Bible) is the greatest success book ever written. The Bible has a theme woven throughout the fabric of its pages... victory in every area of life. The Bible shows us millions of people who had every thing against them, but they came out on top.

What are the principles the Bible teaches, which when applied, guarantees victory in every area of life - every time? Take an in-depth look into the 10 principles that will change your life for the better.

Dear Reader,

You are going to really enjoy this book! It only takes a couple of hours to read it and I believe that you will be encouraged to make some simple decisions that will raise the quality of your life forever.

For instance, on page 38 Terry teaches us the difference between Godly and sensual wisdom. On page 12 we learn the difference between religion and really releasing the power of God in our lives through our personal relationship with Him! But my favorite chapter (the one that is still changing my life) is principle seven: Guard Your Mouth.

I've known Terry's father, LaVerne, since the 1960's. LaVerne used to bring Terry and Robb to my concerts in the 1980"s, when Terry was a teenager. It was obvious in Terry's youth that he was more than a musician and that God had His hand on his life. I've watched him grow spiritually and I am incredibly proud to be his brother in Christ.

Terry has written a book that will build you up, and help you to see how important you are to the Lord and to the rest of us. You are holding in your hand some of the keys to the kingdom of God. Revelation is simply holy information and that's what this book is about. It doesn't matter if you just accepted Christ or you have known Him for 25 years, tomorrow is going to be better than yesterday if you'll simply receive the instruction that God has given Terry for you. The last thing I want to say, other than 'I wish I had written this book', is how much I love, respect and trust Terry Tripp.

May the blessings of God overtake you today,
Mylon Le Fevre

Principle 1

BE THE PERSON GOD CREATED YOU TO BE

Principle 2

LOSE YOUR RELIGION

Principle 3

KNOW WHO YOU ARE IN CHRIST

Principle 4

PUT THE WORD INTO EFFECT

Principle 5

IF YOU FAIL, YOU'RE NOT A FAILURE

Principle 6

SET YOUR MIND FOR SUCCESS

Principle 7

GUARD YOUR MOUTH

Principle 8

PRAY THE PROMISE, NOT THE PROBLEM

Principle 9

REFUSE TO FEAR

Principle 10

GIVE BIRTH TO YOUR DREAMS

Principle 1

Be The Person God Created You To Be

Success doesn't just happen. Victory isn't without a cost. There are decisions made. There are plans laid. There are guidelines to follow. In reaching for the prize, in pressing for the goal and walking in a victorious life, the first thing you must realize is... **you've got to be *you!***

> Difference: Doesn't mean you're less-than or more-than; just different.

God made you unique! You were created in His likeness and in His image. And even though we were all created with the same image and likeness, we all have differences that make us unique. Our society has spent so much time criticizing differences. I think it's time we begin to celebrate our differences, allowing our differences to be the strength where there is weakness.

If God hadn't made you as He did, you wouldn't have been able to persevere as you have. Others couldn't have handled what you've been through. Because of that, you're uniquely equipped to strengthen those around you.

You may say, "Terry, you just don't know, I don't feel unique or perfect enough for God to ever use me in an effective way." **Join the club!** None of us "feels" perfect. That's why we base what we believe by faith and not feeling. God said something about you in His Word that you should always remember,

"You are chosen..."

• 1 Peter 2:9

The word "Chosen" means: to be picked out for special services - to receive special privileges. Think about that! No matter what anyone said about you in your past that formed your feeling to believe you're not special and you'll never amount to anything, God says you are CHOSEN (picked out for special services to receive special privileges!) Since God has said that about you, why would you ever consider what others have said?

"Yea, but Terry I was adopted" or "I was an accident by my mother and dad." Allow me to tell you something about you. You were not born and then God said, "Let me hurry up and figure out what I'm going to do with this life." No! God designed your life and then you were born. Very few people realize they have a predetermined destiny. God has a perfect will for your life. It doesn't matter if you feel like you were a "mistake" or "adopted", or maybe you don't even know who your parents are. The truth still remains, God created you with a predestined purpose and He does not create mistakes. God needed you here because He has something good for you to do.

"For we are His workmanship, created in Christ Jesus for good works, which God prepared beforehand that we should walk in them."

• Ephesians 2:10

You are special! You are unique! You are of God!

I want to encourage you to be the person God created you to be. Do the assignment God has placed in you to do. He went to great lengths to make sure that each of us is an original. We should not feel badly because our personality, tastes, hobbies, or even our spiritual tendencies are not the same as another person. Some people are outgoing and energetic. Others are more laid back. Some wear suits and ties. Others are more comfortable wearing blue jeans. Some close their eyes and lift their hands in worship. Others worship in a more subdued fashion. And guess what? God loves it all! He loves variety!

Warning: In the process of being you, be cautious not to compare yourself with others.

The reason many people are discontented today is because they compare themselves with other people. A friend of mine, who always compared himself to others, asked me what I would think if someone preferred another singer or speaker rather than me. He was going through an identity crisis and couldn't handle the thought of anyone else taking his place, so he was trying to make me feel what he was going through. "Well," I said in a very simple response, "I'm not in a contest."

The Word says, *"Let each one examine his own work."* This means, quit looking at what everybody else is doing and run your own race. You cannot be confident in yourself if you're always comparing yourself to everybody else.

"For we dare not class ourselves or compare ourselves with those who commend themselves. They... are not wise."
• 2nd Corinthians 10:12

There's a situation which took place in 1 Samuel 8:4-20 that shows us the consequences we acquire when we try to copy, and compare ourselves to others. Here's the story:

The quickest way to lose originality is to compare yourself with someone else.

The children of Israel go to Samuel and tell him they want a King over them. Samuel is grieved because he knew that was not God's will. He goes to God and God says to assign a king; although that was not His will. He tells Samuel to warn Israel of what this king will do to them. Samuel goes back and tells them what God said. *"The King will take the best of the land. He'll take a portion of your money, livestock, orchards and vineyards. He'll make your sons and daughters his own slaves."* On and on the warning proceeded. And this is what the children of Israel stated in return:

"We don't care! We want to be like other nations."

Here's the powerful truth I want you to grasp; whenever you try and copy someone else, you are setting yourself up to be a slave.

As much as I love other ministries and would love to be able to teach as great as others, or sing as well as someone else, I am not someone else – I am me and I am the best ME. I learn from others and glean information from others, but I never try and copy someone else. If we make the mistake of trying to copy other people, we're going to be frequently frustrated, we'll waste a lot of time, burn a lot of energy and become a slave to our feeling of inadequacy.

Also, whenever you try and copy someone else, the best you'll ever be is number two. God placed great care in creating you. It would do Him an injustice if you decided not to be who He has created you to be. God created you unique with the intention that you would be the best you, you could be. See yourself as the best... You! It is so important to see yourself that way because your perception will determine the quality of your life. How you see and feel about yourself affects your relationships with other people, as well as your relationship with God.

❖**Perception** - Your best friend or worst enemy

The children of Israel had it all. They had God on their side. Moses was leading them to a great place. They had the wealth of Egypt in their moneybags. They had the promise of God to enter into their destiny, and they had His power to accomplish it. They also had one more thing that totally crippled them from living the life God had for them... **a distorted perception**. They could not enter The Promised Land because they did not perceive themselves the way God said they were. They were not being the people God had created them to be. They said in Numbers 13:33, *"We were like grasshoppers in* ***our own*** *eyes."* God didn't say they were like grasshoppers. He said they were *"well able"* - very equipped to take the land. Ten of the 12 spies Moses sent into the land came back saying, "We were like grasshoppers" and, "Did you see the size of those giants?" Two of the 12 came back saying, "We are well able" and, "Did you see the size of those grapes?" The 10 who came back with the negative report never entered The Promised Land, but the two who saw themselves "well able" entered into the promise of God.

Success is not solely dependent upon your environment. Millions of people have proven you can come out on top even from the most horrible conditions. So your environment, how you were raised and whether or not you had the best education, has very little to do with how successful you can be in life. However, **success is absolutely dependent upon how you view yourself.** If you see yourself as a grasshopper, then you will get walked on and defeated. If you see yourself *"strong in the Lord and in the power of His might"*, you'll be able to overcome any giant in life that would try and hinder you from your... Promised Land!

Always look at yourself through God's Word - His eyes and not yours. In the 10 spies, perception started first in *their* eyes, **not in God's eyes**. If you do not see yourself the way God sees you, it will cripple you from receiving all God has promised you.

Did you see that? Please don't miss that! If you do not see yourself the way God sees you, it will cripple you from receiving all God has promised. No matter what anyone else says, and no matter what anyone else does, you need to see yourself doing what God has called you to do and being who God has created you to be.

My brother, Robb, exemplified this in his life when God

led him to be a pastor. When he told me about what the Lord was leading him to do, I knew it had to be God, because my brother always said he would never do such a thing. His heart was always set on other things. But, after totally surrendering his life to God, he began to see the "Promised Land" (Pastoring a church) the place he knew God had destined for his life. After speaking about "The Promised Land" to some others, he began to face some "Giants" (opposition). He found out not everyone was for him becoming a pastor. He began to receive criticism and conflict from those whom he had once been in close fellowship.

What would he do? Where would he turn? Whose report would he believe? Would he listen to God's report, "You are well able. You are more than a conqueror." Or would he listen to the voices in the wind, "You'll never grow a church here, it's too difficult. Why don't you go elsewhere? You're not trained to be a pastor."

On and on the giants gathered. No doubt, because of the resistance, he probably was tempted to walk away from what he knew he was called to do.

Well, the good news is he chose not to seek for man's opinion, or even man's approval, but he did what he knew God wanted him to do. He set out to be the person God created him to be. Today, their church is growing strong seeing many people saved and restored in life.

Why was he able to do this, even in the face of adversity? Because he knew, to be a success in life, he must be the person God created him to be. He knew if he didn't see himself the way God saw him, then he would not receive all God had promised.

Don't think that you have to fit into somebody else's mold for God to really use you. On the other hand, don't be upset when other people don't fit into your molds. Just be the person God created you to be. I'm not saying that you should do foolish or rebellious things and call it the leading of the Lord. Certainly, we need wise counsel. We never have permission to live an ungodly life. We should never hurt anyone, wound another church or steal a vision from someone else. That's not God's plan or His ways of doing things. But we do have God's blessing to be confident, not letting outside pressures mold us into something we're not.

You are well able!

Yes, you are well able to do all God has placed in you to do. You are equipped with His power (The Holy Spirit) to do all He has called you to do. Right now, while you are reading this book, I want you to see yourself the way God sees you. See who He has called you to be. If you can see it, you will seize it. If you can visualize you doing and being all God has said, soon it will be in the natural. *Your mind creates the map by which your life will follow.* The children of Israel proved that to be true. So did Joshua and Caleb. They made up in their minds they were going to be and do all God had said. Their minds were made up and their lives followed that direction.

Always remember... you are special! God never duplicates; not even a snowflake or a fingerprint. He is looking for originals, not encores. You've been given a fingerprint no one else has. Why is that? Because you've been respectfully and wonderfully made.

Meditate on this all day, "All of God's creation is great. The beautiful fall trees, the winter snow, the spring roses and the gentle summer rain are all wonderful creations, but God's greatest creation, the one He gleans the most joy from is... ME!"

Be the champion you are!

"Your hands have made me and fashioned me."

• Psalm 119:73

Principle 1

BE THE PERSON GOD CREATED YOU TO BE

Principle 2

LOSE YOUR RELIGION

Principle 3

KNOW WHO YOU ARE IN CHRIST

Principle 4

PUT THE WORD INTO EFFECT

Principle 5

IF YOU FAIL, YOU'RE NOT A FAILURE

Principle 6

SET YOUR MIND FOR SUCCESS

Principle 7

GUARD YOUR MOUTH

Principle 8

PRAY THE PROMISE, NOT THE PROBLEM

Principle 9

REFUSE TO FEAR

Principle 10

GIVE BIRTH TO YOUR DREAMS

Principle 2
Lose Your Religion!

If you want to live a complete, free and successful life, you must first, be who God made you to be; and second, develop and nurture your relationship with God. I didn't say find religion. I said, develop a strong relationship. There's a big difference! A well-built relationship with God is the greatest success you could ever have. On the other hand, a religious mindset is the most burdening road you could ever travel.

If someone ever tells me that they are a religious person, I quickly respond with an answer that shocks them...

"Lose Your Religion!"

That's right! Get rid of it. Religion is a lot of rules and regulations that, in all reality, no one can keep. God desires to do good things in and through us, but religion makes us feel like we are not good enough to have such a holy God use us. So, if we can just quit this or quit that, maybe God will accept us. Well, I have good news for you; **God has already accepted you,** just like you are. He takes it all; the good, the bad and the ugly. God knows you better than you know yourself and He loves you in spite of your faults. He knew we couldn't get good enough. That's why He sent Christ into this world to redeem us from the curse of sin. You cannot redeem yourself... That's religion!

What is religion? What is relationship?

Religion: Man's effort to merit salvation as a reward for his own works and behavior. Working to establish your own righteousness is the basis of religion.

Relationship: Because of what Christ did, God takes you just like you are and you can enter boldly, without fear, into His presence and stand as righteous as Jesus.

Religion cannot accept that *Righteous Standing* as a free gift. Religion says if you can do enough, or take off enough makeup, or not go to a movie, or stand near a wall in a certain position and align your spine to the right degree and bow 224 times while you pray, then maybe this will show others, and God, how spiritual (RELIGIOUS) you are.

That is not relationship. That is works. Works is the greatest narcotic known to religion. Every religion - Buddhism, Catholicism, Hinduism, and even some churches and denominations - are works based. True Christianity (Christ in you) is based on His salvation working through you.

Bottom line - **The trademark of Religion is bondage**. You don't have to be bound by religion to be accepted by God. You're already accepted! That acceptance should liberate you to live the life He has assigned and designed for you to live.

While the trademark of religion is - bondage to works, **the trademark of the Spirit is - liberty to live**. Only the

Holy Spirit can set you totally free. Only the life force of Almighty God can liberate you. Not your good works! Only a righteous standing with God through Christ will set you totally free.

> Righteousness is not about your condition, it is about your position.

There is a beautiful story recorded in the Bible. It is found in Luke where Jesus told about a boy who messed up his life so bad he didn't feel worthy enough to go back home to his father as a son. Many religious people would have told that boy, "You're not worthy enough to be accepted again. First, you must clean up your act. You must change clothes, cut your hair, feel guilty enough and acknowledge all the wrong you've done." In that story, you'll notice that the father never even acknowledged the boy's wrong doing. He never told him he wasn't good enough. He didn't tell him to clean up first before he could come home. Even when the boy didn't feel worthy, the father said he was. Though the Prodigal Son's condition was one of failure, his father affirmed his position of son-ship. That affirmation changed his condition.

If drugs, alcohol, anger, pride, jealousy, lust, hatred or anything else binds you... **Religion cannot set you free.** It will simply enforce more rules which will keep you deeper in bondage. Only the Father's love, received by faith, will establish you in a righteous position. As you stand in that position, your condition will change. You will not desire to do the same things as before, because His life will now be in you.

Am I saying you can live anyway your flesh desires because you're under grace and not religious? Absolutely not! Good works are important:

1. They are evidence of our faith
"Faith without works is dead." James 2:26
2. They glorify God and magnify Christ
"That the world may see your good works and glorify your Father." Matthew 5:16

Even Paul wrote to the Galatians and told them not to use the liberty they had received as an opportunity for the flesh, but to walk in the Spirit; **not bound under the law** (Religion), but free in the Spirit. And if they would walk in the Spirit they would not fulfill the lust of the flesh. How could Paul be so certain about them not fulfilling the lust of the flesh? He knew the **power of relationship**.

When you develop a relationship with someone, there is a bond and a trust that's developed. A relationship will cause you to stay true to that person. A relationship places you on a level nothing could ever break. A relationship with Christ gives you something nothing else could ever give, especially religion. That *something* is... GRACE!

We should produce good works. Not to become righteous, but because we are righteous. When you develop a relationship with Christ you're producing righteousness through grace, not works.

You may ask, "Since this is the way it works, how do I build a strong relationship with Christ?" A relationship with Christ is built the same way a relationship with a close friend or even your spouse is built... you invest *time!*

1. Time in His Word
This is where faith is produced. You begin to discover who God is and all He has done for you. In that time, your confidence will grow in God and you'll see just how good He is. There's an old saying that goes, "You become who you hang around." This is true. That's why it's vital you draw close to God and let His love, life and character permeate in you. The closer you are to Him, the more like Him you'll become.

2. Time in prayer
This means you talk to Him, and guess what, He talks to you too. He is not untouchable. Religion makes God untouchable. Turn the TV off long enough to hear Him speak. Don't rely exclusively upon the Pastor, Priest, TV personality or whoever, to tell you what God is saying. You have a direct connection with God, through the Holy Spirit. Use it!

What if your spouse or best friend had to always go through someone else to tell you something? That would get old very quick. God doesn't want to go through others to always get His Word to you. He wants to communicate with you *directly*. That's relationship!

You will never fully experience your rightful place in God if you don't **lose your religion.** What is that rightful place? A son/daughter of God! Religion keeps you as a slave. Relationship places you into the family where there is freedom!

Carl Morris, a friend of mine who Pastors a great church in Florence, SC., sent me some quotes which identify those who might be religious. If you find yourself in any one of these statements, it's time you *lose your religion.*

You might be religious if:

❖You emphasize the external and overlook the internal
❖You do things to be recognized and praised by men
❖You look at what is wrong instead of what is right
❖You've been in 12 different churches in the past 12 years, looking for the "Perfect Church", and left criticizing all 12 churches
❖You have to go outside of your relationship with Christ to find spiritual fulfillment
❖You offer the Lord only that which costs you nothing
❖You are ENCOURAGED when your ministry looks better than others and DISCOURAGED when other ministries look better than yours
❖Your faith is offend-able
❖You have form but no power

Lose Your Religion!

I would like to add one more thing to this list that I've seen in our generation today...

You might be religious if:

❖You seek to achieve a title rather than study to be a servant.

Many people in mainstream churches demand to be referred to with a specific title (Bishop, Apostle, Priest, Saint, Reverend or Doctor). If not recognized with such titles, they can become offended. Please don't misunderstand me, I believe in giving honor where honor is due, but when someone becomes angered when not approached with a certain title, then chances are, they might be religious.

I am reminded of the time my dad, as a joke, tried to get my mom to refer to him as, "lord Laverne." It was quite funny as he justified the title by showing her in the Bible where Sarah referred to Abraham as "lord Abraham." My mother's response was quick and clever. She said, "Well, I'll just remind you, Sarah was 99 when she became pregnant; when I turn 99 years of age and you get me pregnant, I'll call you lord. Until then, your name is Laverne." That settled that conversation.

❖In a relationship, titles are earned
❖In a religion, titles are demanded

Speaking of the Pharisees, who were the most religious sect in Jesus day, Jesus said, *"they love...to have men call them 'Rabbi'"* (Matthew 23:7 NIV). Even in Jesus day, religious people thought, to be important, you must have a title. The truth is, when you build a relationship with Christ, then titles, accolades and the need for others approval, gently fade away. You enjoy being the servant rather than the served.

When given an interview with Billy Graham, Larry King respectfully asked what he should call him. As Larry went down the list of titles, Mr. Graham humbly said, "Larry, just call me Billy."

Here is a man that has sat in the oval office with seven different Presidents. He has seen literally millions of people give their hearts to Christ in his crusades. He has been sought after by the biggest names in Hollywood to give counsel. Yet, he desires to be called "Billy."

A person who is developed in their relationship with Christ has become so secure in who they are they don't need certain titles in front of their name to make them feel more important. Jesus was approachable. Make sure you are too!

I trust you're seeing the importance of building a relationship, rather than being religious. Religion takes away from life, but a relationship with Jesus adds to it (John 10:10).

I will bring this principle to an end with the same thing Paul ended his letter to the Galatians... *"Peace and Mercy be upon those who walk in a* ***relationship****"*... not a religion.

A Relationship with God through His Word is SUCCESS!

Top Seven List of *Religion vs. Relationship*

These are seven things I've heard others say you must give up to accept Christ. In contrast to the religious idea, I have put what relationship offers. I trust this will bring freedom.

Religion –
If necessary, you must give up your health and accept sickness or disease as a test of your faith, believing God is allowing the devil to do this for a special reason.

Relationship –
Because of all Christ did on the cross, we are empowered to receive healing. Don't accept anything less! Isaiah 53:5 *"By His stripes we were healed."* Also James 4:7 instructs us to, *"Resist the devil and he will flee."* Don't accept what the enemy is doing; resist it.

Religion –
You must go through storms to really build your faith.

Relationship –
"Faith comes..." not through storms, but *"by hearing the Word of God."* It grows the same way too.

Religion –
First, you must clean yourself up before God will accept you.

Relationship –
God takes you just like you are. He's the one who does the cleaning. Your part is to be willing to let Him do it.

Religion –
If you're going to serve Christ, you must give up football and all other kinds of sports.

Relationship –
After you've accepted Christ He says, "Take Me to the game with you and I'll show you how to win. At the same time, other people will see the change in you and will desire what you've been given."

Religion –
You must give up fishing!

Relationship –
After Simon allowed Jesus to get in his fishing boat, they caught so many fish their nets begin to break and their boats begin to sink (Luke 5:1-7). Now that's fishing! That's relationship! Take Jesus fishing with you!

Religion –
Don't go to movies! Give up acting!

Relationship –
I believe Jesus would say, 'Make movies about Me that will show the world all I did for them' (The Passion of the Christ).

Religion –
Give up your riches. You must be poor to be used of God.

Relationship –
Jesus says, *"I want to bless you so you may feed the poor, clothe the naked and go into the entire world and preach the gospel"* (Matthew 25:34-40). You can't do all of this if you're broke!

LOSE YOUR RELIGION!

Principle 1

BE THE PERSON GOD CREATED YOU TO BE

Principle 2

LOSE YOUR RELIGION

Principle 3

KNOW WHO YOU ARE IN CHRIST

Principle 4

PUT THE WORD INTO EFFECT

Principle 5

IF YOU FAIL, YOU'RE NOT A FAILURE

Principle 6

SET YOUR MIND FOR SUCCESS

Principle 7

GUARD YOUR MOUTH

Principle 8

PRAY THE PROMISE, NOT THE PROBLEM

Principle 9

REFUSE TO FEAR

Principle 10

GIVE BIRTH TO YOUR DREAMS

Principle 3
Know Who You Are In Christ

One of the underlying causes of poor self-esteem among Christians is a distorted theological perspective. Some believers and preachers focus upon the scriptural revelation of man's sinful, fallen state, stressing the utter worthlessness of man. They mistakenly assume our previous sinful condition has forever rendered us insignificant and valueless before a holy, sovereign God.

They also attack any attitude of self-love or self-esteem as being a form of pride. As a result, they often embrace a false humility, which is nothing more than a demonically-inspired, self-inflicted condemnation.

This distorted theology overlooks the believer's standing in Christ and emphasizes feelings of inferiority and inadequacy. Instead of living in the confident reality of the righteousness of God in Christ, believers fearfully wallow in sin-consciousness.

I once heard a song entitled, "I'm a sinner, saved by grace." I've even heard people in the church make this statement. When I hear it, I want to scream out, "Wait just a minute!" Songs and statements like that will always establish a sin-consciousness. If you've accepted this covenant exchange God laid out for you before He laid the foundations of the world, and you've been washed in the blood of Jesus, I have some good news for you; you're not an old sinner anymore. **You are the righteousness of God in Christ Jesus, saved by grace!**

Remember, this book is for those who desire the God-kind of success. Knowing who you are in Christ is vital to your life, if you want to walk in victory and success.

So let's take a look into the Word and see what it says about who you are in Christ:

"Therefore, if anyone is in Christ, he is a new creation; old things are passed away; behold, all things have become new."

• 2nd Corinthians 2:5

Also 1 Peter 2:9 declares, *"You are a chosen generation, a royal priesthood, a holy nation, His own special people, that you may proclaim the praises of Him who called you out of darkness into His marvelous light."*

First of all, notice what the Word has called you; it says you are a new creation - chosen - royal - holy and special. Where did it say you're an old sinner? It didn't! Saying you're an old sinner saved by grace would be like saying, "I'm just walking in darkness, in His marvelous light." That doesn't make any sense. You've been brought out of slave-ship into son-ship; out of darkness into light. 2nd Corinthians says, *"You are a new creation in Christ!"* Stop identifying with the old you and start seeing yourself as you are in and through Christ:

In Christ - there is no condemnation!

In Christ - you are forgiven!

In Christ - you are God's workmanship!

In Christ - you are valuable and precious!

In Christ - you are pure, holy and righteous!

In Christ - you are brand new!

When you accepted Christ as Savior and Lord, He didn't clean up your old heart, He gave you a brand new one. Why? Because an old heart can't pump new blood. You are a new creation in Christ, not a repair job! You are not renovated like an old building or reconditioned like old furniture. You've been regenerated! That means you've been re-gened! You are no longer connected to the old sinful nature; you've been purchased with a price and brought into God's nature, through Christ. I don't see Him as an old sinner. I don't see Him sick or diseased. He's not in poverty and bondage. **You shouldn't be either!** Until you allow this to permeate your being, the enemy will keep you in bondage to the elements of the curse. That's what he loves to do. If he can't get you in sin, the next best thing to him is to see you weak, defeated, still struggling and barely making it in life. But there's good news. I like how The Message Bible translates what Paul wrote to the Ephesians, *"You who were once out of it altogether are in on **everything**."* (Ephesians 2:13) Everything! He (Jesus Christ) left nothing undone. He made a way to receive eternal life, healing in our body, peace in our mind, joy in our hearts and abundance in every area of life. We got in on everything! Think about that for just a moment. Everything He has, we now have. Not just in Heaven, but NOW!

When you come to the place and recognize all Jesus did for you, and you see all He has made you to be in Him, your entire belief system changes. You begin to believe for the best. You believe for bigger and better things. You don't accept that old-sin nature anymore, nor do you accept those things that accompany the sin nature; bondage, disease, poverty and depression. Once you discover who you are in Christ, there are no limits to how successful you can be!

I want you to realize who you are in Christ. I want you to live life on the premier level. I want you to see yourself the way God sees you. He does too! He wants you to see yourself the way He sees you.

How does God see you?

Did you know God sees you as a joint heir with Christ? Romans 8:17 says, *"And if children, then heirs - heirs of God and joint heirs with Christ."* When you are a joint heir with someone, and you receive a large inheritance with him or her, you'll change the way you think. You'll live life on a different level.

In a natural will, to be a joint heir means you share in all the benefits, riches, land, cars and inheritance with the other sibling. You might have been broke and in debt up to your eyeballs, but when that certain person died, the will came into effect and carried you onto another level of living. You went from not enough to more than enough.

When Jesus shed His precious blood on the cross and died,

God's will came into effect and carried you into another level of living. You are now a joint heir with Christ! You have been redeemed out of everything that pertains to death and the kingdom of darkness, into all that pertains to life and the kingdom of light, which includes healing, prosperity, benefits, riches and the same anointing Jesus (the anointed One) has. That's who you are... a joint heir!

Now I ask you, how can you think broke? How can you think sickness or disease? How can you think depression? Jesus paid too high-of-a-price for you to think any other way than... VICTORIOUS! He suffered too much with those stripes upon His back for you to live no other way than healed. He took upon Himself poverty so you could be made rich. It would be an injustice if we lived any other way.

Now, please don't misunderstand me. I do not want to put anyone down who may be in such a predicament - sick, diseased, broke or depressed. I want to build you up and let you know God has provided the way out! You may say, "Terry, I'm not walking in victory. I'm still sick. I'm still broke. I'm depressed. I'm still just barely making it. What can I do?"

What I am about to give you is going to set you free. I believe with all of my heart this will be the answer to what you've been praying and believing for. **Get ready!** Here is the key:

Lay Claim To What's In The Will!

When a person dies, their inheritance doesn't just fall into the heir's lap. The heir has to *lay claim* to what's in the will. They have to show up at the appointed place and say, "That's me, that's mine and I'll receive it. Thank you very much!" There are certain procedures an individual must do in order to receive what is rightfully theirs.

The same thing applies when it comes to the WILL of God. You must go to the appointed place (HIS WORD). Go to that Word and lay claim to what is yours. Speak the will out loud with your mouth. When you see, *"By His stripes ye were healed"* then say, "That's for me, that's mine and I receive it. Thank you very much!" When the Will says, "You are a new creation in Christ" lay claim to it. When you see, "He has made us more than conquerors" then don't settle for anything but winning in life.

You are the healed! You are the righteous! You are above and not beneath! You are a champion! That's who you are in Christ. **Lay claim to it**. It's in The Will. God sees you that way. Wouldn't you think it's time you see yourself that way?

Some people may say, "You are teaching that you should work for your inheritance. It's not by works, it is through grace." That's true. I agree. It is by grace. Yet, there is a procedure you must operate in to receive what has been provided by grace. God's not just going to force it on you. For instance, the moment you heard the message of salvation you were not born again. You were born again only when you laid claim to The Will. You were born again when you looked at The Will, saw the procedure it took to become born again and then did accordingly. What was the procedure? *"If you confess with your mouth and believe in your heart that God has raised Christ from the dead, you will be saved"* (Romans 10:9). It wasn't your works that saved you, but you had to operate in the procedure. You had to make the choice to lay claim to what was already provided in the will.

In the same way, in order to rise up and become all you are in Christ, you must go to The Will (The Word of God), find out who you are and then begin to lay claim to it. You have been made a joint-heir. You got in on everything Heaven has to offer! Now lay claim to it and receive it. It's already yours.

As if that weren't enough, you're not only a joint-heir, but you are also a king and a priest. Revelation 1:5, 6 says, *"...To Him who loved us and washed us from our sins... has made us* ***kings*** *and* ***priests*** *to His God and Father..."*

As a king, we should walk in authority and have dominion over the situations of life. Dominion means: the right and the power to govern and control. We don't control people. That's witchcraft. We exercise dominion in the earth over life's problems, instead of life's problems having dominion over us.

As a priest in Christ, we can boldly walk into the presence of God and receive strength, wisdom and direction for our lives and the lives of others. As a priest, we are to minister to the needs of others.

Did you know you were made all of these things in Christ? The moment you confessed Jesus as Lord and Savior of your life He declared you as royalty, a king and priest, righteous, holy and more than a conqueror. That's who you are. Now act like it! Lay claim to it! Honor the Lord by being who He has made you to be. Be a person of love and character. Be a person of your word. Be a person who is always willing to serve and to demonstrate a royal-priestly attitude toward others. Not with pride, but with love.

I trust this principle has opened your eyes and has helped you to see all you are. Look in the Word, and anytime you see "In Christ" or "Through Christ" read it carefully because you will discover another part of who you are. When you see it, lay claim to it and say, "That's for me, it's mine and I receive it."

Four Things To Affirm Daily

1. The blood of Jesus has cleansed me from all unrighteousness; therefore, all sin-consciousness, guilt and condemnation are under my feet. (1 John 1:9)

2. I have abundance of grace in my life that empowers me to live righteous. I rule in life because of The One, Jesus Christ! (Romans 5:17)

3. I make a decision to lay claim to all of my covenant benefits God has provided for me through His dear Son Jesus Christ. (Psalm 91)

4. Today, I see myself the way God made me to be. I am strong in the Lord. I am free from condemnation. I am highly favored. And I am healed, whole and victorious!

"Let this mind be in you which was also in Christ Jesus..."

• Philippians 2:5

Principle 1

BE THE PERSON GOD CREATED YOU TO BE

Principle 2

LOSE YOUR RELIGION

Principle 3

KNOW WHO YOU ARE IN CHRIST

Principle 4

PUT THE WORD INTO EFFECT

Principle 5

IF YOU FAIL, YOU'RE NOT A FAILURE

Principle 6

SET YOUR MIND FOR SUCCESS

Principle 7

GUARD YOUR MOUTH

Principle 8

PRAY THE PROMISE, NOT THE PROBLEM

Principle 9

REFUSE TO FEAR

Principle 10

GIVE BIRTH TO YOUR DREAMS

Principle 4
Put The Word Into Effect

If you want to enter a level of blessing that many of the world's most celebrated successes know nothing about... put the Word into effect. The Word is powerful! Yet, many are not living in victory like the Word says they can and should.

With all of the various kinds of religions in the world, different denominations and big theological seminaries all giving their interpretation of scriptures, I will have to admit, it can become a challenge to rightly divide the Word and make it all useful. We must have the Holy Spirit guiding us. The Word of God is actually simple.

When you get right to the heart of the matter, there are only three things you need to put the Word into effect. That's right! Three! Although simple, they are powerful things that will always put the Word into effect.

What are they?

These three things *define* the line that separates those who walk in freedom, from those who forfeit their opportunity.

What are they?

They are...

Faith! Wisdom! Action!

Let's study these three things.

1. Faith

The requirement for pleasing God is faith. You may say, "Great! But what is faith?" First of all, sight is not faith and feeling is not faith. Faith believes before you see, hear or feel, and it often goes against your feelings. Faith is to believe what we do not see in the natural, and its reward is to see and enjoy what we believe. Faith expects from God, when all natural circumstances hold no expectation.

"Now faith is the substance of things hoped for the evidence of things not seen."

•Hebrews 11:1

Faith is the substance. That means it's the "title deed" to whatever you believe for. **When you have the title deed to something you have every right to claim it as yours.** It's yours no matter what anyone says. God's Word (The Bible) is your "title deed" to every covenant promise He has given to you.

Don't look to the natural! Faith operates in the realm you cannot see, and what is in that realm, through the seed of faith, is birthed into the realm you can see.

Faith is the evidence of things not seen. How can you have evidence of something you can't see? You must walk in the spirit. That means to see it in the spirit. Faith operates in the spirit, not in the head. **Faith perceives as real truth, what is not yet revealed to the senses.**

Many people become discouraged when they don't see things happen immediately in the natural. Everything that happens in the natural happens first in the spirit. For instance, when you speak healing for your body, I believe instantly your spirit receives it. As you keep applying God's Word in the area of healing, very soon your soul (mind, will and emotions) will take hold of it, and then you will see the manifestation of it in your body. The reason many good-hearted people never receive healing is because they become discouraged. Instead of continually speaking the Word, they allow natural circumstances to weaken their faith and confession.

Never allow faith to be moved by natural circumstances, move natural circumstances by faith.

Now that we've established what faith is, you may be asking, "How does faith come?" Faith comes one way. **Hearing God's Word**. It's that simple. If you're not hearing the Word, you're not building faith in the Word. You don't have to be some special preacher, teacher, pastor or priest to receive faith. The only requirement you must have to get faith is an ear to hear.

"Faith cometh by hearing and hearing by the Word of God."

•Romans 10:17

The Lord birthed faith that produced the Promise through Abraham by this principle of *hearing The Word*. Author and teacher Charles Capps gives a good explanation regarding this principle. He says, "When God told Abram he would be 'Father of nations' it was a challenge for that old man and his wife to accept. So, in His infinite wisdom, God changed his name from Abram to Abraham; which means, "Father of nations." Every time he (Abraham) heard his wife call him by name, he heard the promise of God, "Father of nations." He didn't necessarily hear the name Abraham; he heard the promise, "Father of nations." And guess what happened, **faith was birthed**. Every time one of Abraham's servants called him "lord Abraham" he didn't hear that, he heard "Father of nations" "Father of nations" "Father of nations."

For many years Abraham heard the promise of God and his faith was established to such a degree that he believed, accepted and made up in his mind, "I am father of nations." Even when the natural said, "No you're not, you're a 75 year-old man and getting older." Abraham considered not his own body; he just believed God and it was accounted unto him for righteousness. The promise came into fruition by hearing and believing God's Word." (End quote)

Do you see the process? Abraham received the promise in his spirit. The more he heard **The Promise**, not the problem but the promise, the more real it became to him. He then received it in his soul (mind, will and emotions) and then the manifestation came in the natural.

The more you hear God's Word and accept what He has already said about you, the more substance (faith) is birthed and produced. That substance is the title deed to every promise God has given and brings those promises into effect in the natural realm.

You must get in the Word! You cannot give your attention to the world and expect to receive the promises of God. Here's why. Whatever you give your attention to is what you will magnify. Whatever you magnify you will manifest. Whatever you're putting faith in is what you'll receive in your environment. So get in the Word. Give your attention to that! Magnify that! His Word can take you from faith to faith (full to overflow). Get in the Word!

2. Wisdom

Have you ever heard the statement, "Knowledge is power"? It's true. Wisdom is the most prized possession to have on earth. Joseph obtained it, David possessed it and his son Solomon had it. God Himself created the heavens, the earth and all that is in it with wisdom (Pro. 3:19). Do you know why wisdom is so important? *Your faith can only operate on the level of your knowledge.* If we don't understand how something works, we will never get to enjoy all that it has to offer. Some are never healed because they don't know what The Word says about healing. Some never prosper because they have no wisdom regarding prosperity. You must have wisdom concerning God's Word or it will not work for you.

Where does wisdom come from? How do we receive this wisdom that is declared to be better than rubies, gold, silver and riches? Proverbs 4:7 says, *"Wisdom is the principal thing, get it."* Get it! There's not a lot of gray area there. It's black and white. Get wisdom and get understanding! Why is the writer so adamant about us getting this wisdom? Because it puts The Word of God into effect.

Let's look at what the Word says about wisdom and how we can obtain it. It's yours for the receiving so... "Get it!"

Wisdom vs. wisdom

Did you know there are two kinds of wisdom?

❖Godly

and

❖Sensual

First, let's look at the sensual. James 3:13-15 *"Who is wise and understanding among you? Let him show by good conduct that his works are done in the meekness of wisdom. But if you have bitter envy and self-seeking in your hearts, do not boast and lie against the truth. This wisdom does not descend from above, but is earthly, sensual, demonic."*

Sensual: psuchikos (psoo-khee-koss);

- ➢ Belonging to the natural or physical
- ➢ Unspiritual
- ➢ Earthly
- ➢ The sense realm

This wisdom lives in the domain of the five senses, moved and influenced with only what it sees, hears, tastes, touches and smells. This kind of wisdom can go no further than what the natural allows.

Have you ever asked someone how they were doing and they responded, "Good, under the circumstances." That's their problem; they're living "under the circumstances," just like so many others live "under the circumstances." They use (psuchikos) natural wisdom. This wisdom is not sufficient enough to out wit spiritual attacks, storms in life and problems that come their way. Of course, you can survive for a while, but before long you'll be under, instead of soaring over them.

Paul warned the church in Ephesus not to walk in the realm of the sensual. He said,

"This I say, therefore, and testify in the Lord, that you should no longer walk as the rest of the gentiles walk, in the futility of their mind, having their understanding darkened, being alienated from the life of God..."

• Ephesians 4:17, 18

When you walk in the realm of the sensual, it's dark. The same verse says, when you operate your life according to the natural, you are alienated from the life of God. What does that mean? That means you no longer walk in the realm of revelation. You are now limited to information. Whoa! Did you get that? When you are alienated from the life of God (The Word), you are bound solely to information and cut off from revelation. Darkness follows! You *must* have the light of God's Word, which renews your mind and empowers you to live a victorious life (Ephesians 4:23).

We've briefly looked at the sensual. Now let's look at the God-kind of wisdom and the results we can expect to receive as we apply this kind of wisdom into our lives.

This kind of wisdom is called: Sophia (Sof-ee-ah)

- Comprehensive insight
- A right application of knowledge
- Insight into the true nature of things

Wisdom (Sophia) is having the insight of God and seeing things the way He does.

How do we get this wisdom?

"For the Lord gives (Sophia) wisdom; from His mouth come knowledge and understanding."

• Proverbs 2:6

This (Sophia) wisdom comes from the Lord's mouth. What is His mouth? His Word! His Word and time in His presence produces (Sophia) wisdom (Insight into the true nature of things).

It doesn't just happen! You don't just wake up one morning and have the wisest mind in the universe; you must renew your mind according to The Word. Many people say they just don't **have the time** to get in The Word. Those same people, as you get to know them, **make the time** to watch CNN a couple of hours a day, listen to tales and fables and read all of the gossip magazines. As soon as a crisis hits their lives, all of the sudden they wonder why God isn't coming through for them the way they think He should.

• Ignorance is not inherited, it is learned •

Now, I'm not saying it's wrong to watch CNN, the weather channel or a good movie, but when you need direction, when you need to be building yourself up on your most holy faith, the last thing you need to be doing is filling your spirit with fear, doubt and unbelief. My point... don't expect your house to weather the storm when you've not invested the time to build it upon the rock.

You have to seek!

"If you receive my words, treasure my commands, incline your ear, apply your heart, cry out, seek and search as for silver and hidden treasures; then you will understand."

• Proverbs 2:1-5

You must get in His Word and seek for wisdom and understanding as if you were seeking for costly treasures. If someone handed you a map for a hidden treasure worth billions of dollars and you had confidence in this person, knowing that what they said was true, what would you do with that map? I'll tell you what you would do. You would do everything you could to find that treasure worth billions of dollars. You wouldn't lay the map on the coffee table and think you know where the treasure is. Nor would you rely upon someone else to tell you where the treasure is. You've got the map! You would want to use it to know exactly where to go.

If you'll do this with a map to obtain a hidden treasure, then why not with God's Word to obtain wisdom? God cannot lie! He said if you would seek for wisdom like hidden treasures you would find it. He's given us the map to abundant life. "Abundant" means: Excessive, too much and more than enough. Think about that for just a moment. God has given us a map (His Word) to create a life that's better than we could have ever imagined; too much life, excessive healing, too much favor, too much increase, excessive joy and more-than-enough money to do all He would have us to do in this life. Praise God!

So, quit being lazy with it! Get into it! Wisdom comes to those who seek. And when wisdom comes, you will know how to apply the Word of God in every situation of life. His Word works if you understand how to work it. Get wisdom!

3. Action

Let's suppose you had a classic car in your garage, and you had all the faith in the world in that car's ability to drive like a cherry. You could have all of the wisdom and knowledge about that car. You could know the complete history of that old car. You could show everyone where the gas line connects to the cylinder, where the spark plugs go and what lines connect to make the car run as fast as it could. All of those things are great, but if you never make the decision to put the key in the ignition and put that car in drive, it would never take you anywhere.

Many have faith in God's Word. A lot of people have wisdom on how His Word *can* work. There are hundreds of Bible Colleges that give you insight and knowledge on The Bible, and all of this is great. I know people who can quote hundreds of verses at a time, could tell you the date the verse was written and who wrote the verse; but they never walk in the victory The Word can bring. They never put the key in the ignition and go! You can obtain all of the faith and wisdom in the world, but if you do nothing with them, you'll receive nothing from them.

Let this be the moment you make a quality decision to do more than just have a theological knowledge of The Word. Allow this to be the defining moment in which you will not stay motionless in your walk with God. Put action to The Word! Faith requires action!

"Faith without works is dead"

• James 2:26

If you want to live life to the fullest, and experience victory over every situation, then it is vital you add works to your faith. I, personally would say, it is imperative you apply action to The Word. When you apply the principles, you receive the promises.

Put the Word into effect with these principles - Faith! Wisdom! Action!

Start Here:

Put The Word First
The value and importance you place upon The Word will determine how you respond to it; the way you respond to it will determine how you are rewarded. One of the biggest excuses the enemy will give you is that you don't have enough time. If you keep waiting until you have enough time, you'll wait for the rest of your life. You must come to the place that His Word means life to you. Solomon said that wisdom is the, *"Principal thing."* Principal means *"First in importance."* That means

the Word of God needs to occupy the place of highest importance in all of your activities.

Select a system

Don't just read at random. Create a method. You may want to start with a chapter of Proverbs every day, or set a goal to read the entire New Testament in 37 days. You can do this by reading seven chapters a day, which would take approximately 30 - 35 minutes a day. Select a system that is good for you. This is half the battle. *Remember, you will never leave where you are until you know where you want to go.*

Don't rush it

Even though I said to set a goal, don't get in a hurry. Our goal is not to see how much we can read in the shortest amount of time. Our goal is to take in the very life of God through His Word. We receive the "mind of Christ" in and through His Word. So, enjoy every minute of it. The Word is God's DNA. Take time to get it inside of you.

Treat the Word like your most prized possession. When you invest your time in the Word first, that investment will soon pay off in every area of your life. You will discover success like you've never dreamed.

The Word!

Hear it...

Speak it...

Live it!!!

Principle 1
BE THE PERSON GOD CREATED YOU TO BE

Principle 2
LOSE YOUR RELIGION

Principle 3
KNOW WHO YOU ARE IN CHRIST

Principle 4
PUT THE WORD INTO EFFECT

Principle 5
IF YOU FAIL, YOU'RE NOT A FAILURE

Principle 6
SET YOUR MIND FOR SUCCESS

Principle 7
GUARD YOUR MOUTH

Principle 8
PRAY THE PROMISE, NOT THE PROBLEM

Principle 9
REFUSE TO FEAR

Principle 10
GIVE BIRTH TO YOUR DREAMS

Principle 5

If You Fail, You're Not A Failure!

Nearly all people who strive for success make a mistake along the way. You must realize every great person that has accomplished great things was given the opportunity to fail in their attempt. The decision whether to accept failure, or reject it and move on, is what determined the final product.

If I were to ask, "Name a great baseball player." Who would you name? There are so many; Sandy Coufax, Pete Rose, Henry "Hank" Aaron, or everyone who loves baseball knows of Babe Ruth. He hit 714 home runs. He held the title of "home run king" for many years. Did you know that he struck out 1,330 times? He hit 714 home runs, but struck out 1,330 times. Babe Ruth failed, but he was not a failure.

How about Football? There have been many great quarterbacks; Joe Montana, Joe Namath and John Elway. I like Terry Bradshaw because he has a great first name. Terry led his team to four Super Bowls. Yet, Terry Bradshaw threw more incomplete passes than any other player who ever played the game. Terry Bradshaw failed, but he was not a failure.

If I were to ask you to name a great president, I believe one would come to mind; Abraham Lincoln. Do you realize he lost eight elections? He failed in business twice and had a nervous breakdown. Abraham Lincoln failed, but he was not a failure.

The great discoverer of electricity, Thomas Edison, had many opportunities to give up and accept defeat. During his many attempts at achieving a goal which would effect the way we operate the entire world as we know it, people would come up to him and say, "Boy, you really failed that time didn't you." He would simply say, "No! I just discovered another way it wouldn't work." When given the opportunity to become a failure, he didn't accept it.

These men didn't major on their mistakes; they majored on their goal. They didn't focus on what they couldn't do, but on what they could do.

You're not a failure just because you failed in accomplishing great things in the past. You're not a failure! Champions do make a mistake. Making a mistake doesn't make you a failure. **The way to become a failure is to sit and settle in your mistake.** If and when you do make a mistake, **don't settle!** Don't look at certain situations, which ended up with different results than you expected, as opportunities to accept failure. View them as another way it didn't work, and then move on to what does. Get up and try again!

As long as there are people in this universe, you will have the opportunity to accept defeat, failure and other opinions on your situation, but do what Jesus said do... *"Cheer Up!"* Why should we be of good cheer? Because we're not playing a nine-inning game. **We play until we win!** It's a fixed fight and you've already won. So never accept failure. Life for you is not over. You are not washed up, or too old. You have not made too many mistakes!

If you feel like a failure and you always confess, "I'm just a failure," then you're calling God a liar. He said, *"You're above and not beneath, the head and not the tail, more than a conqueror and blessed (Empowered to prosper) in all you do."* See yourself that way!

What does religion say to a person who has made a mistake? Religion says, "Well you failed, so you need to sit down for two years so we can see, and evaluate just how sorry you really are."

God doesn't have to consult your past to determine your future.

I want to take you to The Word, and show you a disciple of Jesus, a Christian, and a son of God who made a mistake and had the opportunity to accept failure.

The Garden of Gethsemane has happened. Judas has betrayed Jesus. Jesus has been arrested, and now He is at the house of Caiphus, the high priest. Jesus is on trial. The Apostle Peter follows at a distance and in Mark 14:66-72, we find him denying ever knowing Jesus.

Peter, for three years, walked with Jesus, heard the sermons and saw the miracles. Jesus healed his mother-in-law. Peter saw Jesus at the Sea of Galilee and said, "Lord, if it's you, bid me to come," and Peter walked on the water. He was there at the tomb of Lazarus, and at the Mountain of Transfiguration he heard the voice of God say, "This is my beloved Son in whom I'm well pleased." But, Simon Peter denied even knowing Jesus. Peter failed. He made a mistake. He dropped the ball – missed the pass.

What did Jesus do? Did He say, 'Alright, now sit down for two years until you learn your lesson?' Or, 'Sit down so we can see just how sorry you are and then we will evaluate your case to see if you're fit to be an effective preacher.' Sad to say, this is how a lot of religious organizations handle those who make a mistake.

Is this how God did it?

Let's take a look at how God responded to the man who cursed and denied Him. It's Sunday morning. The tomb is empty. Jesus has died. He's been buried. He's been raised. The women go, looking for the body of Jesus and the angel appears. I love what the angel says in Mark 16:7 *"But go tell His disciples and Peter."* Have you ever wondered why the angel singled out Peter? Think about it. Why didn't the angel say, 'Go tell His disciples and John, or James, Andrew or Philip'? He singled out Peter. Why? Think about it. Why Peter of all people?

It's as though the angel was saying, 'Peter, (I want you to know that) just because you made a mistake, Heaven does not believe you're a failure.' 'Tell Peter (though) he struck out, he gets to bat again. Tell Peter that just because he threw an incomplete pass, he doesn't have to sit on the bench. Go tell His disciples, and Peter.' Peter was not a failure. He didn't sit down on a bench and quit. He was sorry, he wept bitterly, **but he got up**, squared his shoulders back, and in weeks, not years, but weeks, he preached a message to the Jews and converted 3,000 in one day (Home run!!!)

He was the one that said in Acts 3:6, *"Silver and gold have I none; but such as I have I give to thee; rise up and walk."* The man leaped up and began walking, rejoicing and praising God. Peter used that miracle as an opportunity to deliver yet another sermon which converted a few thousand more. Peter might have failed when he denied Jesus, but according to the Word, he wasn't a failure. Why? Because he didn't give up!

Maybe you have denied God. Maybe you've used God's name in vain, been addicted to alcohol or drugs, gone through divorce, experimented with homosexuality, had an abortion, or whatever!!! No matter where you've been or what you've done, there is hope for you. Look at what Jesus did after Peter swore he didn't know Him, after he cursed Him and denied Him. The Word says in Luke 22:61 *"Jesus turned and looked at him."* I don't know what you see in those eyes of Jesus, but here is what I see:

I see LOVE!

When you make a mistake and mess up so bad, and you look into the eyes of Jesus, what do you see?

I don't see eyes of anger, I see eyes of acceptance!
I don't see eyes of bitterness, I see eyes of benevolence!
I don't see eyes of criticism, I see eyes of compassion!
I don't see eyes of exasperation, I see eyes of expectation!
I don't see eyes of guilt, I see eyes of grace!
I don't see eyes of hostility, I see eyes of hope!

I hope you will not sit and settle in your mistake. You can rise up to be the champion He sees you are. It's not too late.

Judas Iscariot made a mistake. Simon Peter made a mistake. The difference: one settled - the other didn't. One accepted failure - the other didn't.

> The only way you'll die a failure is if you make a mistake and then settle.

What if Babe Ruth would have quit after the first strike? He would not have been known as one of the greatest baseball players of all time. What if Terry Bradshaw would have just given up, sat on the bench and quit after the first incomplete pass? He would not have four super- bowl rings in his possession. If Abraham Lincoln had accepted failure after the first election he ran in, millions of slaves would not have walked free. We would not be enjoying the convenience of lights, computers, air conditioning, cars, airplanes, and so much more had Thomas Edison given up on his 1,201 attempt.

If you do make a mistake, go for the gold... again! Don't settle! You're not a failure! Don't accept the opportunity to be one. Rise up! Be the success God has created you to be.

You Are A Champion!

Principle 1

BE THE PERSON GOD CREATED YOU TO BE

Principle 2

LOSE YOUR RELIGION

Principle 3

KNOW WHO YOU ARE IN CHRIST

Principle 4

PUT THE WORD INTO EFFECT

Principle 5

IF YOU FAIL, YOU'RE NOT A FAILURE

Principle 6

SET YOUR MIND FOR SUCCESS

Principle 7

GUARD YOUR MOUTH

Principle 8

PRAY THE PROMISE, NOT THE PROBLEM

Principle 9

REFUSE TO FEAR

Principle 10

GIVE BIRTH TO YOUR DREAMS

Principle 6
Set Your Mind For Success

For many years it was believed that no human could run a four-minute mile; it was scientifically stated, "Physically impossible." Yet, Roger Bannister, shattered this belief when he ran a 3:59 mile. How did he do it? **He set his mind!** He repeatedly visualized his triumph so intensely that his certainty gave a command to his physical body and he achieved the results to which his mind was set. Following in Bannister's stride and believing that they, too, could do it, within one year several others duplicated his feat.

"Nothing can stop the man with the right mental attitude from achieving his goal; nothing on earth can help the man with the wrong mental attitude."

❖ President Thomas Jefferson

The way you think determines your personality, character and destiny.

Wrong thinking produces wrong believing. Wrong believing produces wrong actions. And wrong actions produce wrong results.

The best way to develop a victorious attitude - which is key to living a successful life - is through God's Word. If you'll begin now giving your attention to the Word of God and the things of God, you'll develop such an attitude for victory and success that nothing will ever get you down.

I didn't say you wouldn't be tempted to get down. As long as you're in the natural, you'll be faced with storms, tests and problems, but someone who has developed a victorious attitude through God's Word knows that you can rise above these things.

It's your decision

Everyday you get up, you have a choice regarding the attitude you will embrace. You cannot change the past and you cannot change the fact that people will act in a certain way. The only thing you can do is decide how you respond with your attitude.

You may say, "Terry, you just don't understand what I'm going through. There have been layoffs at my job and I could be next. How can I keep a positive attitude and set my mind for success when I'm worried?" If that's the case, then tell me, what good does it do for you to worry about something that hasn't happened yet? First, thank God you have somewhere to work right now, and even if they do let you go don't get discouraged. Just say, 'Thank you Lord, I know you've got something even better for me and I thank you for giving me the opportunity to be Your example at this job.' With a smile on your face and an attitude of confidence, work as if they were considering giving you the next promotion, not the next layoff. A person with an attitude for success keeps a smile on because they know they will be rewarded from God no matter what; *"My God shall supply all of my needs according to **His riches** in glory by Christ Jesus."* I'm glad the Word didn't say, "According to the boss' riches?" It said, "His riches" (God's riches! Your Father's riches!) This means no matter what, you're taken care of. He is not laying anyone off. He's only handing out promotions to those who seek Him and *set their mind* on things above. There is no shortage in God's economy. You're a successful child of God.

But you must do your part! That's right! It doesn't just happen. Promotion and blessings aren't given to lazy and stubborn children. God's power cannot function in someone who doesn't work on the job with honesty and integrity. I really want you to grasp what I am writing to you here.

His blessings are falling down all around you like a flood of rain. Now, do your part. What's your part? Your part is to set your mind to work harder than the world does on the job. Your part is to show honesty and integrity, even when no one is watching. It is your responsibility as His example to show the world that Christians aren't lazy and we don't complain about the pay, the boss or the way things are done, no matter how much we may disagree. We show honor. We walk in love. We have a better attitude at work, church, business and home than anyone else. To be successful, realize it takes work. If it were easy, everyone would be successful. It takes a determination. It takes a willingness to change and an effort to stay focused.

"Set your affections on things above, not on things on the earth."

• Colossians 3:2

Whatever direction you set your mind is the direction in which your life will go. The word *affection* is the word *mind* in some translations. SET YOUR MIND. Notice where the responsibility lies... US! It's our job to set, not God's. He's already done His part and has given us the power to do ours, but we must *set our minds* to do it.

That leaves this question, "How do I set my mind?" The same way you set the alarm clock. You say, "I'm going to get up at 6:00 am." No matter what's going on in the world, you set the alarm - you plan to get up. Do the same thing with your mind. Set your mind in the direction you want to go with your life. If you want to prosper, set your mind there and forget about what everybody else says. People will talk about you when you decide to move your life forward. If you want peace, joy, and goodness - the Bible says you should *set your mind* that way. No matter what's going on in the world, set your mind and your flesh will hear the alarm, then respond accordingly.

Often we assume that it's because a person was born the right color. Some think you must go to the right college or you must be a genius to accomplish something great in your life. Some feel that age and weight are essential to really experiencing success. Although going to a good school and putting forth an effort to look and be your best is important, the fact still remains...

"As a man thinks in his heart so is he."
• Proverbs 23:7

In pertaining to how a person lives and walks through life, this is the most powerful verse in the Bible. Think about it; as you think, you are. Do you ever wonder why some people are so shy and others seem like they could take on the world? The reason why is because they think that

> You will never be more than what you dare to think and you will never do more than what you dare to think.

way. Do you ever wonder why some people get so angry at little things? They think that way. Some feel so insecure. Why? They think that way. Some say, "I can't." Why? They think that way.

Quit thinking you're nothing. Stop thinking you can't and **set your mind** to, *"I can do all things through Christ"* (Phil. 4:13). Quit thinking doubt, worry and fear and **set your mind** to, *"God has not given me the spirit of fear, but power, love and a sound mind"* (2 Timothy 1:7). Quit settling for a poverty mentality and **set your mind** to, *"I am blessed in the city and blessed in the field. I am blessed when I come in and blessed when I go out. Everything I place my hands to is blessed. I shall never be without because I am above only and not beneath, the head and not the tail"* (Deuteronomy 28:3-13).

You may say, "Well, I just can't help the way I think. I've been set in my ways for so many years. I've been trained to think this way. It's too late for me to change how I think."

That's not true! It's never too late. "But Terry, other people have set my mind for me." Not true! You're the only one who decides how you're going to think. Others may try and influence you, but ultimately the choice is up to you.

You're also the one who changes your mind. No one else can change it for you. And yes, you can change it.

A gentleman called a church one time and asked the secretary, in an old southern expression, if he could speak to "the head hog at the trough." The secretary responded in an upset voice, "Sir, if you are referring to my Pastor, I am offended and I don't appreciate that at all." He responded by saying, "I meant no disrespect. I just wanted to make a $50,000.00 donation to the church." The secretary replied, "Sir, hold on. Porky just walked in."

See, this funny story proves you can change your mind... Quickly, I might add. You can change your mind and you can *set your mind* to think in a certain way.

Who sets the alarm clock? You do. Who sets your mind? You do. Just like there are directions for setting an alarm clock, there's a system for setting your mind as well.

What's the System?
The Law of Harvest!
Whatever you Sow, you Reap!

Look at this powerful scripture as it pertains to the mind through the system of seed and harvest:

"For those who live according to the flesh ***set their minds*** *on the things of the flesh, but those who live according to the spirit, the things of the spirit."*

• Romans 8:5

Whether you realize it or not, this verse shows us the powerful law of seed and harvest. Allow me to paraphrase this verse to make my point a little clearer:

"If you sow the seed to set your mind on the things of the flesh, then your harvest will be to walk according to the flesh; but if you sow the seed to set your mind on the things of the spirit (The living Word of God) then the harvest will be to walk and live (be led) by the spirit of God."

> The seed you're allowing to be sown into your mind is influencing the way you set your mind.

So, I ask you to think for a moment about the seeds you've been sowing into your soul (mind, will and emotions). Have those seeds been flesh-inspired or Spirit-inspired? Were those seeds produced by what you saw on television, heard on the radio, read in a gossip magazine or from the mouth of another person, or were they brought about by the living Word of God?

How does a thought enter the mind?
There are three gates to your soul (mind).

1. The eye gate
2. The ear gate
3. The mouth gate

Whatever you allow yourself to see, hear and speak are seeds that influence the way you set your mind. If you invest all of your time watching things that promote anger, violence and murder, those are seeds being sown.

Whether you are aware of it or not, **you** are setting your mind in that direction. Don't be surprised when someone cuts you off in traffic and your reaction is to want to hunt them down, tear their face off and mail it to their momma. Why? Because your mind has been set in that direction. You've sown seeds that have produced that harvest. Don't wonder why it may be a challenge to remain faithful in a relationship, after you spend time listening to music that endorses lust and adultery. Don't wonder why it's a challenge to enter into praise and worship at church the way you should, after you've been out partying the night before. Why? Because the system of harvest is working. You reap what you sow.

So, what do you do?

"Set your mind on things above." Sow the seeds of seeing, hearing and speaking God's Word. When you do this, your harvest will be, *"...the mind of Christ."* The spirit of God will lead you when you put on the mind of Christ.

In order to live life the way it has been made to live, you must learn to control the thoughts that enter your mind. You must learn to train your mind to think in line with God and not the world.

How do you do that...?
Re-program your mind!

We are living in a world that is bombarded with fear, doubt and worry. It seems everywhere you turn there's a major tragedy being broadcast. Our minds have been programmed by all of this. That's why it's so important we reprogram our mind.

If you're familiar with computers, you know that someone has to program it before it will function. A computer will only do what it is programmed to do. Well, in a sense, our minds are the greatest computers ever made. God put it together with memory banks in which to hold or store certain information. Just like the computer, your mind will only do what it has been programmed to do.

For example, if you have always been in a negative environment and people have been critical, then you probably deal with being negative and critical yourself. But the good news is, you can take the Word of God and re-program your mind. You can take the Word and replace your old way of thinking with a brand new VICTORIOUS main frame.

Now I'm not saying you will never be tempted to think about certain things that don't line up with God's Word. The enemy, every chance he gets, will always try and install a "virus" in your memory bank. What do you do in those times? Do what the Word says do, *"...cast down evil imaginations."* Treat those thoughts as you would a bird. I can't help if a bird flies over my head, but I don't have to allow that bird to set up a nest on my head and start a family. Don't entertain a thought that goes against the Word. Capture that thought and cast it back down to where it belongs. Delete it from the memory file and never go recycling for it again.

I believe if you'll make a decision, right now, to set your mind towards a victorious life, you'll find yourself there very soon. If you'll program your mind with thoughts of the Word, you'll grow and mature in love to such a degree you'll overcome every obstacle on your way to success.

Always remember how powerful the law of seed and harvest is. It works for everyone everywhere.

Roger Bannister applied it in his life. He sowed the seed of thinking he could go one mile under 4 minutes. He set his mind in that direction, watered the seed with work and his natural man produced the harvest of the thought (seed) sown.

I want to encourage you today to stay positive in whatever your plans may be. Set your mind on good things (God's Word). Hear it, see it and speak it. As you do, realize you are sowing the right seeds and you are setting your mind towards the successful life God has created you to live. Choose now, no matter what, you will set your mind for success through God's Word.

The following chapter just may be the most important chapter you'll ever read. Thinking positive is very important. Yet, thinking good-positive thoughts only change you. The way you think affects you. If you desire to see circumstances change, your thinking is not what changes them. The way you think changes how you respond in regard to the circumstances, but it doesn't change the circumstances. You must have a greater power than thoughts to change circumstances.

Is there such a power available?
Is there such a force on hand to create any environment we choose?

YES!

Thoughts change you!
Words create and change environments!

Thoughts are extremely important and powerful, but **words are a creative force.** God didn't think, 'Let there be light.' He **spoke**, *"Light be, and light was"* (Hebrew translation).

Proceed to the next chapter and discover the power of your words.

Principle 1
BE THE PERSON GOD CREATED YOU TO BE

Principle 2
LOSE YOUR RELIGION

Principle 3
KNOW WHO YOU ARE IN CHRIST

Principle 4
PUT THE WORD INTO EFFECT

Principle 5
IF YOU FAIL, YOU'RE NOT A FAILURE

Principle 6
SET YOUR MIND FOR SUCCESS

Principle 7
GUARD YOUR MOUTH

Principle 8
PRAY THE PROMISE, NOT THE PROBLEM

Principle 9
REFUSE TO FEAR

Principle 10
GIVE BIRTH TO YOUR DREAMS

Principle 7
Guard Your Mouth

"He who guards his mouth preserves his life."

•Proverbs 13:3

What if, in the next 12 hours, you received everything you said? Immediately! Would you monitor what you spoke? Would you be cautious about what you were going to say and how it would affect others around you? Would you guard your mouth from all things negative? Would you be more conscious about using words that would construct a more positive environment? Whether you realize it or not, sooner or later, you will have what you say.

To live a success-filled life and to walk triumphant over the disasters and storms in life, you must grasp this truth... words are spiritual containers. They have power! Words have the power to start wars or create peace, destroy relationships or strengthen them. Words create how we feel about certain people, situations and life. The words you select to describe a person or situation immediately changes what they or it means to you and thus how you feel. Words guide and place you at certain locations at appointed times; whether you were aware of it or not.

You may feel like words are not that important. What if you were to share with me a deep conviction and I tell you, "you're mistaken!"? What if I say, "you're wrong!"? Worse, what if I choose to use the words, "You're lying." Will this affect our interaction? I think so! Why? Because words create an atmosphere. Words construct environments.

In the Bible, James said, *"If any man seems to be religious, what he believes will be in vain if he doesn't watch what he speaks."* There are many that seem to be religious, but they don't bridle their tongues. This costly mistake holds many born again believers in bondage. Too many people speak all sorts of things that destroy their faith and deceive their hearts. Little phrases such as, 'My legs are killing me' 'I'm just dying to go' 'Tickles me to death' 'Scares me to death' or 'I'm taking the flu', come pouring forth from their vocabulary. When some are made aware of it, they change. Others say, "Well, God knows my heart, He knows what I mean." After speaking those little phrases and then saying, "God knows what I mean" would be like you dialing up your friend on the phone and getting the first three or four digits right and the next ones wrong and saying, "The phone company knows what I mean." If you want to make a successful phone call, you must use the method it takes to do it. If you want to live a successful life, you must use the method it takes to do that.

Why do we need to be conscious, as the body of Christ, about the words we speak? Ephesians 4:29 in the Amplified Bible says, *"Let no foul or polluting language, nor evil word nor unwholesome or worthless talk [ever] come out of your mouth, but only [speech] as is good and beneficial to the spiritual progress of others, as is fitting to the need and the occasion, that it may* ***be a blessing and give grace*** *[God's favor] to those who hear it."*

This verse shows us that words create environments. We should know this because of Genesis chapter one where "God said". He used His words to frame His world. And guess what? **Your words frame your world.**

Words Create

Words created your body. Words can heal your body. Words can also keep your body sick. Medical science discovered a few years ago what the Word of God has said for thousands of years. They have discovered that about seventy percent of all sickness comes from what people say or do. There are some doctors and neurosurgeons using the power of words as a form of therapy. For instance, if someone has high blood pressure then they urge that patient to speak this for 15 minutes a day, "My blood pressure is a hundred and twenty over eighty." These same doctors have said, "Whether or not the patient understands what they are saying makes no difference; their body knows and will obey them."

You may ask, "I just don't know how this can work?" Allow me to take you to the Word and show you how. *"For assuredly, I say to you, whoever says to this mountain, 'Be removed and be cast into the sea,' and does not doubt in his heart, but believes that those things he says will be done, he will have whatever he says."* (Mark 11:23)

This is not mind over matter. This is God's Word over all matter. God told Adam to have dominion, and that dominion was through his words. You have the same ability to reign in life as Adam had, through your words.

Words are the most powerful thing in the universe. They will work for sinner or saint. Words show no prejudice. It doesn't matter what color, race, religion or age you are, words work the same way for everyone.

Christians who are defeated in life are defeated because they believe and speak the wrong things. Yes, they are born-again and on their way to heaven, but they are living defeated here on this earth. Why? They speak words of doubt, worry and death to express how they feel, without even realizing it. They speak words of the enemy, and those words hold them in bondage.

> *"...Thou art snared by the words of your mouth."*
> • Proverbs 6:1, 2

Also, words not only can hold you in bondage, but they also can hurt others. Have you ever heard the expression, "Sticks and stones may break my bones but words will never hurt me"? **That's a lie!** Words can hurt, not only hurt, but some words, if spoken at the wrong time, in the wrong way and to the wrong person, could eventually kill. How is this possible? Words go down into the inward part of a person. For instance, when a parent speaks words over a child, or to a child, they are literally shaping the future of that child. If the parent speaks words such as, "You're not good enough. You're never going to make it. Why don't you just give up? You're ugly! Why can't you be more like your brother or sister?" Those words are like seeds planted into the heart of that child and if left to grow and flourish, could harvest a life full of failure, defeat and ultimately an early death.

Do you see now how words can kill? There's another expression I've heard which goes along with this, "Stop shooting off at the mouth!" It makes sense - especially when you look at Psalm 64:3 and see how David compared words to arrows. The wicked, he said, *"sharpen their tongues like swords and aim their words like arrows."* In the same way you can't retrieve an arrow after it's been released, you can't reverse words after someone is hurt. Next time you're tempted to, "Shoot off your mouth," stop and consider whether your words may become "deadly arrows."

Just like our words can bring about failure or even death to a life or an environment, in the same way our words can bring about victory, hope and life. Begin now to verbalize blessings over your household, wife, children and entire family. Lift them up! Be the voice of hope and love in their lives. This will result in an atmosphere charged with the presence of God because He is life.

You may say, "Terry I've done that. Now, my children are grown, they're making decisions on their own and it doesn't seem like the words I've spoken are working." Let me remind you, when you put a seed in the ground, just because you don't see it working, doesn't mean it's not working. If you placed it in the ground and **didn't dig it up**, I can assure you, the laws of physics can assure you and the law of seed and harvest can assure you, **the seed will produce a harvest.** When you don't see it working and it looks as if the harvest is not coming, that is not the time to quit speaking words of faith, hope and love. That's the time to stand strong and know His Word will not return void. It will accomplish what it was created to do. The seed is working in the ground - harvest is on the way.

Words Govern Life

(1)During the Gulf War there were two soldiers. Both were females and were being sent to Saudi Arabia as part of Desert Storm. Before they left for Saudi Arabia, they were interviewed. Being women serving on the front lines, so to speak, was noteworthy. One of the soldiers said, "You know, I just can't help believing that I'm not going to make it back," and this became her pattern of speech. The other soldier interviewed said, "Well you know, I'm looking forward to getting over there and getting the job done and getting back," and this became her pattern of speech. One soldier had a positive confession about her life and the other had a negative.

They were in Saudi Arabia in the technical end of what was happening and were in a huge barracks area. While in the barracks one night, one of the soldiers (the one with the positive confession), couldn't sleep and kept tossing and turning. Finally, she got the urge to get up and she went outside to take a walk along the grounds to get some fresh air to help her sleep. Her walk took her from the compound and the barracks. She had gotten a little distance away, still within the perimeters of their security, when a scud missile, fired from Iraq, landed in the center of the barracks she had just left. The soldier who had made the confession that she probably wouldn't come back, died in that explosion. When the incident was over and the media recapped the entire story, the two women were consistent in maintaining their pattern of speech, with one positive and the other being negative. One lived and came back home, **just like she said.** One died and never returned home, **just like she said.**

Words Release Angels

We must realize something extremely important about words. They can release the ability of angels or they can release the ability of the enemy. When you give voice to the Word of God in faith, it releases the ability of angels. When you give voice to fear and death, it releases the ability of the devil. Angels work inside of the perimeter of your words. When you talk about yourself in terms of death and dying, negatively, the angels are powerless to help you. The only time angels can defend you and do what they've been called to do, which is to minister on your behalf, is when you speak the Word, when you give voice to the Word. Speaking the Word of God over, or into your circumstance or situation, gives the angels something to work with. God has commissioned angels to respond to His Word no matter if it comes from His mouth, my mouth or your mouth. His Word employs them.

Your Body Responds to Words

A leading neurosurgeon told a friend of mine that the speech center in the brain exercises dominion over the entire central nervous system. He went on to say that this was a recent discovery of medical science. He also said you could cause different parts of the body to respond with stimuli from corresponding parts of the brain. When the speech center is stimulated, the whole central nervous system responds so much, that when a person says I am weak, the speech center sends out the message to the whole body to prepare to be weak. This must be the reason why in Joel 3:10, God said to tell the people, *"Let the weak say I am strong."* God created this body with such precision and awe. He knew **if they would speak His Word into their situation, their situation would line up with those words.**

Producing Increase With Words

An acquaintance of mine told me of a man he once trained in sales. He said this man was the most unlikely person to sale anything. He didn't have the look, the talk, the walk or the gift it took to sell what the company was offering. He was doing this as a favor for the guy. So, he trained him and then sent him off on his first day. He flopped! For three weeks nothing happened. Not one sale! The requirement was to sell three items a day; this man wasn't selling even one a week much less three a day. He just wasn't "Qualified". Then the man did something uncommon. He took a piece of paper and wrote the number 1 on it. He placed it on the dash of his car and the next time he left to go and present his product he said, "Thank you, Lord, for my one sale today." Guess what? He got the sale. For that entire week he would look up on the dash of his car and see that number "1" and say, "Thank you, Lord, for my one sale today." For one solid week he sold one a day. The following week he changed the 1 to a 2 and began to say, "Thank you, Lord, for my two sales today." Every day that week he sold two a day. Guess what happened next? The 2 became a 3 and again the same results. Today, the number 6 is on that card and every day that gentleman, who didn't have what it took to be a salesman, is now closing six deals a day and he credits it to, "Thank you, Lord, for my six sales today." He guarded his mouth! Instead of complaining and becoming discouraged about what he wasn't doing, instead of focusing on not being "qualified" for the job, instead of stopping after the first week and giving up, he began to praise and give thanks to the Lord for his desired results. Every day, he doubled the requirement needed for the company. Now the company seeks out the man who wasn't "cut out" for this job to train other sales people.

His words changed his environment

Since words govern our lives, influence our family, employ angels, effect our bodies, and create our environments, I humbly submit to you that People need to stop saying things which do not agree with God's Word, such as: "I'm over the hill," "My memory is going," "My eyesight is going," and "My hearing is going." People talk about getting old long before they ever get old. Now, I understand they do it because it's funny and everybody gets a kick out of it. They do it because that is what they have heard their entire life. It is easy to get caught up in old traditions. But this book is for those who desire to live victoriously, who want to live a long life filled with good days, who desire to have their *"youth renewed like the eagles"* and who want success in every area of life. To have all of those things it is vital to **guard what we say**.

Oprah Winfrey was interviewing Sir Anthony Hopkins, an Oscar-winning actor. She asked him this question, "Do you ever get caught up in the character you're playing? And does the character you're portraying ever have an effect on you physically?" His response showed me that the world even recognizes the power of words. He said, "There have been times when I have become caught up in the character I play. As I have become older I now realize I have to be cautious about how many times I do certain scenes. If I repeat the same scene over and over, my physical body begins to respond because it doesn't know the difference from acting or from real. All it knows to do is **respond to what I'm saying or doing**." He went on to say, "In my last movie there was a scene in which my character has a heart attack and I would only give them two takes because if I repeat that scene again and again, my body will soon respond to what I am saying and doing." (End Quote)

Jesus said in Mark 4:26-29 that our words are like seeds. Whether you realize it or not, eventually, you will have what you say. In the natural, some seeds take root and begin to produce a harvest overnight. Others take months and even years to grow into fruition. But make no mistake about it, you will receive a harvest from every seed you sow, and so it is with what you say. There may be times when you are tempted to say something which doesn't agree with God's Word. This is the moment when you must **guard your mouth** and think of the consequences your words will bring.

Now, don't live on eggshells. If you do make a mistake, repent and then speak words of faith, hope and love into that situation. You will have what you say!

True winners have been those who have mastered their words instead of their words mastering them. Top corporate organizations have seen that *positive words help create a positive environment.* Think about that for just a moment. They have spent millions of dollars to discover what the Bible has said all along – *Words create your environment* (Mark 11:23). They have recognized that if you'll master your words, you'll master your environment. How much more should a child of God be a winner in this life!

Your conversation reveals whether you are winning or losing in life. Winners speak of the possibilities - Losers major on their problems. Winners focus on opportunities - Losers focus on obstacles. Winners talk like victors - Losers talk like victims. Winners have an idea - Losers make excuses.

Wake up! Guard your mouth! Change your speaking! Stop speaking like a loser. You've been made to excel in life and win over every circumstance. You'll only win if you talk that way. You can speak words of the enemy and create problems, or speak God's Word and create solutions. As you guard your mouth from speaking the things of this world, and train it to speak God's words, your world will be re-created.

> Change your words and you'll change your environment.

Realize, the gift of speech is for more than just mere communication, but rather to sow seeds and construct the environment in which God has destined for us to live. I want to encourage you to stop using words to describe your life and start using words to design your life.

Prophecy to Your Circumstance

Throughout the entire Bible we see God training people to use their words to change situations. I think of Ezekiel in Ezekiel 37:1-4, The LORD had shown him a valley full of dry bones. These bones represented the children of Israel at that time. God asked Ezekiel a question, *"Can these bones live?"* Now listen carefully to Ezekiel's response. It's what most of us say when we are faced with circumstances we feel is beyond our control. He said, *"Oh Lord, You know."*

Doesn't that sound like some of us? "Lord, only you know if this situation can work out in my favor. Lord, only you know if healing is for me. Lord, only you know if my family will be saved. Lord, only you know if my finances will get better. Only you know. Only you know." Those type of statements sound very religious and dependent upon God. The truth of the matter is we are waiting for God to do something He has empowered us to do. He didn't say to Ezekiel, 'Good answer' He said to Ezekiel, "**You** prophesy to the bones." In other words He was saying, 'Ezekiel, **you** change the situation. I've given you My power and the words to say, but you're the one that must release the life.'

Notice: Ezekiel didn't talk about the dry bones. He didn't say, 'Oh, Lord, the bones are so dry. There are so many bones in the valley. I just don't see how this situation can change.' No! He prophesied as the Lord commanded him. The Lord didn't command Ezekiel to talk 'about' the situation. He commanded him to prophesy 'to' the situation.

Many people talk *about* their situations, instead of talking to them. Instead of magnifying the sickness in your body, prophesy healing to it. Instead of magnifying how your children aren't serving God, prophesy the Word over them. Instead of magnifying how dry your checkbook is, prophesy the life of God's Word into it. Whatever is drying up around you, speak the life-giving Word of God into it.

God used this method at the beginning of Genesis. He spoke what He desired, not what He saw, and it appeared. If you don't like what you see, (dry bones in a valley) debt, sickness, family problems, etc., speak what you desire, according to God's Word, and your desire will be formed.

Sometimes Silence Is Effective

In Joshua chapter six, God wouldn't allow Israel to say a single word the entire time they encircled Jericho. The reason for this unusual request can be easily understood when you look back on Israel's history of murmuring and complaining. Forty years earlier they allowed the 10 spies with an evil report to persuade them to speak against God's promise. They slandered the land and thereby cancelled their ticket to enter into God's promise which flowed with milk and honey. Therefore, God made sure this time they wouldn't even get the opportunity to talk their way out of the victory. He, in essence, told them to keep their mouths shut until they heard the ram's horn and then shout for the Lord had given them the city.

There will be times in life when you'll be faced with certain situations you may not know how to handle. In those situations, if you don't know what to say, keep silent until you get the Word on the scene (in your heart). When that happens, SHOUT the victory. Don't softly whisper. Shout for what is rightfully yours. Why? Because you have an enemy trying to steal all God has for you. You don't deal with an enemy in a sweet and nice way.

If someone was in your house robbing you and you walked in on him or her, how would you voice your authority?

Would you quietly and softly say, "Excuse me, would you please leave?" Of course not! You would demand with a tone of power, "Get out... NOW!" The same applies when dealing with the forces of darkness who are trying to steal all God has blessed you with. Place a demand, with a tone of authority, on what is yours.

On the other hand, when dealing with people, whether it is on the job, at church or in life, it's vital we heed to the verse in Proverbs which says, *"A soft answer turns away wrath."* When the pressure is on, it's easy to allow emotions to get involved and be tempted to scream your point. But what good does that profit anyone? I've noticed people are much quicker to go out of their way for you when addressed with a tone of love and respect, rather than a tone of dominance and arrogance. This goes for conversing with your spouse and children as well. When you keep a tone of love, you'll be amazed at the wonderful and rich environment created in your home.

What would happen to the way you feel if you consistently thought about dealing with various challenges in terms of "I am above and not beneath" rather than "struggling to keep my head above water"? Would you feel different about taking a test if you talked about "sailing" through it rather than "failing"? Would your perception of time change if you talked about it "flying" rather than "crawling"? Absolutely!

When I became aware of how important words are, I broke some habits in my vocabulary. Now that you see just how vital this principle is, you may ask, "Terry, how do I acquire a more positive vocabulary?" Here is what I did... I **replaced my words**.

What words do you use to describe the things you do every day? How do they make you feel? What would be your environment should you get what you said immediately? Would it be death, sickness, the flu, job loss or lack of money? What new words could you use to be more effective and make life more enjoyable?

I've heard you can form a new habit in just 21 days. Let's do it! For the next 21 days monitor what you speak. Be aware of the words you speak and how, if they were to come into being immediately, they could affect you, your loved ones or your environment.

Three Steps to a New Environment:

1) Write down seven words, metaphors or phrases you regularly use to describe yourself, others and certain situations. Are they somewhat uninspiring?

2) Come up with seven new words or phrases that will absolutely change your environment for the better. For instance, the next time you begin to feel certain symptoms, instead of saying, "I'm trying to take the flu" which will only send you one direction... to the flu, replace such a statement with, "I receive my healing in Jesus name."

How many other positive life-giving words could you use to design a life more enjoyable to you? Make a list now.

3) Enlist the aid of three people who will hold you accountable. I'm not talking about people who are going to thump you over the head if you say the wrong thing, but those who will lift you up and remind you of the right things to say.

For the next 21 days replace those seven words or phrases with new ones. You'll begin to see changes in how you perceive things. You'll notice a difference in your environment. I'll guarantee you one thing, the people around you will be happier you did this, because no one likes to be around the debris of death, fear and negativity. Replace that trash with the life-giving Word of God. Speak it and live in success!

(1) From the book "Long life and Good days" Author Dr. Les Brown

Principle 1

BE THE PERSON GOD CREATED YOU TO BE

Principle 2

LOSE YOUR RELIGION

Principle 3

KNOW WHO YOU ARE IN CHRIST

Principle 4

PUT THE WORD INTO EFFECT

Principle 5

IF YOU FAIL, YOU'RE NOT A FAILURE

Principle 6

SET YOUR MIND FOR SUCCESS

Principle 7

GUARD YOUR MOUTH

Principle 8

PRAY THE PROMISE, NOT THE PROBLEM

Principle 9

REFUSE TO FEAR

Principle 10

GIVE BIRTH TO YOUR DREAMS

Principle 8
Pray the Promise, Not the Problem

Have you ever stopped and listened to some of the prayers that are prayed? Not all, but some are so filled with doubt, worry and fear. Something like, "Oh God, I just don't know how I'm going to make it. I've got this mountain in front of me and I just don't see a way out. Will you please move it for me?" In those three short sentences we were able to establish these four things: Doubt, Worry, Fear and Laziness. This type of prayer produces only one result... defeat. Why? Because all we did was major on the problem. It's okay to identify the problem, but if you want to have a successful prayer life, if you desire to live victorious and strong over every circumstance, don't magnify the problem; rather, magnify the promise.

Put God to His Word!

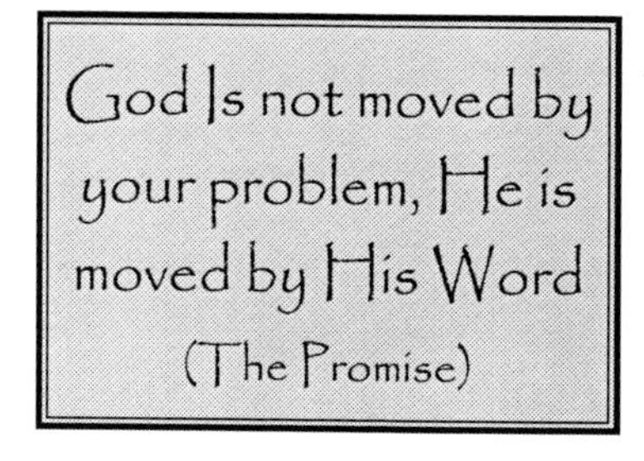

When you study the life of Jesus, you find several important facts that caused Him to overcome the world, the flesh and the devil. I want to give you two of them:

1. He spent much time in prayer, but He never prayed the problem; He prayed the answer. God's Word is the answer.

2. He always spoke the end results. Never did He magnify present circumstances. He spoke the desired results.

"I tell you the truth, if anyone says to this mountain, be cast into the sea, and does not doubt in his heart but believes that what he says will happen, it will be done for him. Therefore I tell you, whatever you ask for in prayer, believe that you have received it, and it will be yours."

• Mark 11:23, 24

Notice, Jesus didn't deny that mountains exist. He simply said when you are faced with one -- when you are faced with circumstances or problems in life that appear to be, as big as mountains, *don't tell God how big your mountain is, tell the mountain how big your God is!* Speak His Word (The desired result) into that situation and live in victory.

Today, you have a choice to either magnify faith or magnify fear. **Whatever you speak you are magnifying.** Your words carry power! We saw that in the previous chapter. Use that power to create what you desire. If you desire a better job, begin to thank God for that better job instead of wasting energy complaining about the one you have. Perhaps you have just been fired. Do not give in to majoring on feelings of rejection. Instead, point out the possibility of a promotion to a better job and changes of freedom which suddenly may emerge. If the doctor has just reported to you that you have arthritis, instead of magnifying the arthritis, magnify the author and finisher of your faith. He said by His stripes you were healed. If you were, then you are! **Magnify that!**

Why should you be so cautious about what you magnify? Because, whatever you magnify becomes greater. Anything you place under the magnifying glass becomes bigger. Anything that proceeds out of your mouth (The Magnifier) becomes superior in your life. Pray the promise and magnify the success of God's Word for your life.

That is exactly what Peter and John did in Acts 3 after they were arrested and were commanded not to preach or teach in the name of Jesus.

"And being let go, they (Peter and John) **went to their own company,** *and reported all that the chief priests and elders had said unto them. And when they heard that, they (the whole company)* **lifted up their voice** *to God with one accord (they prayed), and* **said, Lord, thou art God...**"

•Acts 4:23, 24

There are two key points in these verses:

1. Peter and John went to their own company

When storms come your way, it's very important the company you keep. You cannot allow just anyone to come inside your house and begin speaking into your life. You don't need someone in your house, looking outside your window and giving you a weather report – telling you how dark and hopeless your situation looks. You don't need someone telling you the horrible thing that happened to so and so when they faced the same situation you're facing.

"They went to their own company."

When storms come, surround yourself with people who only speak the Promise. People who will say, "Let's get God's plan on the matter." People who know how to pray! People who refuse to even look at the natural circumstances, but choose to place God's Word as final authority!

2. They said, Lord, thou art God...

All of those people gathered together in one accord and didn't begin their prayer by talking about the problem. They didn't put the problem first. They put God first. They didn't start praying about the mess they were in and what a fix they were in because Peter and John had gotten arrested.

They said, "Lord, THOU ART GOD!!!"

No matter what happens, **He is still God**. No matter how dark it looks or what kind of mess it looks like you're in, God is still God!

Over every sickness, He is Lord.
Over every disease, He is Lord.
Over every financial need, He is Lord.
Over my family, He is Lord.
Over my children, He is Lord.
Over my church, He is Lord.
Over my country, He is Lord.
Over everything that pertains to this life...

JESUS IS LORD!!! Glory to God!

No matter what you're facing right now, when you pray, start your prayers with the solution! The solution is His Word and His Word is forever. Also, believe you receive when you pray. Notice the Word didn't say to believe you receive after you pray, or when you see the manifestation of prayer; no, it says, *"**when** you pray, believe you receive and you shall have"* (Mark 11:23, 24).

I want to give you three keys that will unlock the door to getting your prayers answered. When you apply these, you will see results!

3 Keys to Effective Prayer

Key #1
Make prayer a life attitude

It's not something you do just over your food or on Sunday to begin and end the service. Don't pray just when you want something, or only when you're in trouble. Pray, to commune with the Father. Make it your way of life.

Would you take a few minutes and be mindful of the presence of God and talk to Him from your heart. Develop a relationship with Him. You'll love the results.

Key #2
Pray to release power

Prayer is the only avenue in which we can exhale the spirit of man and inhale the spirit of God. Now that's power! My grandfather said that prayer is the most powerful tool on earth. He prayed for my dad for 15 years to accept

Christ. When it looked like there was no hope, he prayed. When my dad wanted nothing to do with God, he prayed. When my dad would have rather had a drink or a drug than to hear about Christ, my grandfather prayed and victory followed. My dad now stands preaching the gospel of Christ, totally delivered from drugs and alcohol. Through his ministry, more than 500,000 people have accepted the gift of salvation. It's all due to one thing... a father's prayer.

- Prayer can birth deliverance - Philippians 1:19
- Prayer can save a city - Genesis 18:16-32
- Prayer can heal the sick - James 5:15

Do not quit praying for that loved one or friend, even when it looks hopeless, because **prayer releases power.** You have authority as a believer. You have all of Heaven behind you. Use that authority by opening your mouth and praying. You have the power to dispatch angels by one thing; prayer. You have the authority to bind and break every generational curse by one action; prayer! You have the right to loose and speak blessings over you and your household by the supremacy of prayer. Use it to release power!

KEY #3
Make prayer a daily habit

Daniel prayed three times a day. David said, "seven times a day I praise you!" Even Jesus, so often, went away from the crowds to commune with the Father.

Set aside a place where you meet with God every day, just you and Him. You will be uplifted, regenerated and equipped to do with excellence the assignment God gives you. You'll learn more in an hour with Him, than you'll learn in a lifetime with anyone else.

Don't live without it!

Below are some Scriptures to pray over your life. I am giving you these scriptures because many have made statements like, "Lord, just whatever you will, let it come to me." This can be dangerous praying because the enemy will attack you and you'll just accept it because you'll assume it's God's will for your life. To pray specifically and accurately, you need to know the will of God for your life. His Word is His will. If you don't know it, then not knowing it could destroy you.

"My people are destroyed for lack of knowledge."
• Hosea 4:6

Find the will of God that pertains to your situation, then make your stand on it and proclaim it. Pray these Scriptures which magnify the promise, and then live in the victory:

Prayer for family's salvation:
"Lord, thou art God over my family. All in my household are saved. This year I see everyone in my family sitting at the table of the Lord, feasting upon Your Word." (Acts 16:31, Matthew 9:10)

Prayer for healing in your body:
"Lord, thou art God over my body. I believe I receive healing in my body. I choose to magnify Your Word over the negative report. I choose to magnify Your Word over how I feel in my body. I walk by faith! I am a Covenant child of God and in that Covenant there is healing. It's mine in Jesus name." (Isaiah 53:5)

Prayer for guidance and direction:
"Lord, thou art God over my mind. I ask according to James 1:5 for wisdom. I believe that I receive it generously from You because You will not withhold any good thing from me. I have the mind of Christ as I yield myself to the leading of the Holy Spirit. I commit to following You as You direct me into all Truth." (James 1:5, 6, Matthew 7:11)

Prayer for deliverance:
"By the authority of the written Word of God, and in the victory of Jesus Christ's shed blood; I bind, rebuke, and bring to no effect all curses that have been placed against me. I break the power of negative words. I break all generational curses. I break and render useless all prayers not inspired by the Holy Spirit, whether psychic, witchcraft, or counterfeit tongues that have been placed against me. I am free! For whom the Son sets free is free indeed! No weapon formed against me shall prosper!" (Revelation 12:11, Matthew 16:19, John 8:36)

Prayer for finances:
"Lord, thou art God over my finances. You are my source! I don't look to my job, or the government, or my boss. I am thankful for them, but You and You alone are my source. I am the righteousness of God in Christ Jesus and

the righteous have never been forsaken nor left out in the cold to beg for bread. Thank you, Lord, for providing me, my family, my church and all who are connected to me, with abundance. At the end of the month we have more than enough left over to sow into every good work."
(2nd Corinthians 5:21, Psalm 37:25, Matthew 6:25-33)

Always remember: *Don't use prayer to describe your problem, use it to create solutions.*

Some people criticize this kind of praying because they feel as if you're bossing God around. You're not bossing God! God commanded us to bring Him into remembrance of His Word. Obeying His commandment does two things:

1. It builds our faith as we hear our confession of His Word
2. It honors God because we believe His Word

When you pray this way you're simply sowing seed God has furnished from His Word. God is Covenant-obligated by His own Word to perform it. That Word will not benefit you unless you place a demand on it (See Principle three again - Lay Claim to The Will).

Sow The Word into your spirit (heart, soil) and then expect a harvest. You reap what you sow! Sow The Promise, not the problem!

Prayer

I believe, as we agree, you receive all God has provided through His dear Son, Jesus Christ. Take a moment, write down what you're standing in faith to receive and mail it to our ministry. My wife and I, our partners and this entire ministry, will lock our faith in agreement with the two verses below and expect God to intervene on your behalf.

"Let us come boldly to the throne of grace, that we may obtain mercy and find grace to help in time of need."

• Hebrews 4:16

"If two of you agree on earth concerning anything that they ask, it will be done for them by My Father in heaven."

• Matthew 18:19

Terry,

Be in agreement with me for the following:

____

____

____

____

____

____

____

____

All information is confidential.

Tear out this page and mail it to:
Terry Tripp Ministries
P.O. Box 899 - Gallatin, TN - 37066

Principle 1
BE THE PERSON GOD CREATED YOU TO BE

Principle 2
LOSE YOUR RELIGION

Principle 3
KNOW WHO YOU ARE IN CHRIST

Principle 4
PUT THE WORD INTO EFFECT

Principle 5
IF YOU FAIL, YOU'RE NOT A FAILURE

Principle 6
SET YOUR MIND FOR SUCCESS

Principle 7
GUARD YOUR MOUTH

Principle 8
PRAY THE PROMISE, NOT THE PROBLEM

Principle 9
REFUSE TO FEAR

Principle 10
GIVE BIRTH TO YOUR DREAMS

Principle 9
Refuse To Fear

What would you attempt to do if you knew you couldn't fail?

This question, my mother had engraved on a beautiful silver block, sits in my office. Fear paralyzes many from fulfilling their God-given purpose in life.

In Luke, Chapter 19, a wealthy businessman entrusted his entire estate to three key workers. He gave the first five talents, the second two talents, and to the third he gave one talent.

Now when you realize that in Bible days one talent was about a 15-year salary, you begin to grasp what an opportunity this was. It was a defining moment which gave each individual the opportunity to:

1. Demonstrate stewardship
2. Apply good judgment
3. Profit from their investment

And two men did exactly that, but the third was bound by the spirit of fear (afraid of failing). He decided to "play it safe." So he buried his talent. Note; he wasn't judged for what he did; he was judged for doing nothing. In fact, Jesus called him *"wicked and lazy!"*

Fear of failure will always make you want to bury your gift. Unless you have the courage to start, you're already finished! When God called people like Moses, Jacob,

Noah and the twelve disciples, they all had to overcome, not deal with, but overcome fear. So will you! Fear of poverty made Jacob deceive his father. Fear of starvation made the Israelites want to run back to Egypt. Fear of men made the disciples forsake Jesus in His darkest hour, and it made Peter deny Him - three times!

What has fear made you do? Or, another way to ask... what has fear kept you from doing? You cannot afford to fear. Fear tolerated is faith contaminated.

In my book, *Unlocking God's Formula for Successful Living,* fear is described as:

False
Evidence
Appearing
Real

Did you get that? The evidence only appears to be real. It's not real unless you operate on that level. What level? The False-Evidence level. This area goes against what God's Word has said. The way you operate on that level is to accept the lie of the enemy. The enemy tries to get you to look at the false evidence. He knows whatever you give your attention to you will magnify and what you magnify becomes greater. If he can get you to magnify the natural circumstances or the false evidence, then those things will become greater in your life. So, when he presents to you false evidence that does not line up with God's Word, don't accept it. Refuse to fear! Refuse to let it stop you from standing on God's Word! Refuse to give in to doubt and worry!

Have you ever wondered why you worry? Think about it! Why would you ever fear? I'll tell you why... a lack of trust in God. If you really trusted Him, there would be no room for fear and worry. I want you to realize how big your God is. He will never let you down. Even if you're in the wilderness He can make a way for you to live victoriously.

Have you ever stopped to consider how He provided for the children of Israel forty years in the desert? If left to only natural ability this would have been an impossible task, but God provided for them everyday. Let's take a look at what was needed for close to three million people to live:

1. Food

They had to be fed. Feeding this many people required a lot of food. Moses needed 1,500 tons of food a day. This would fill two freight trains each a mile long. Remember, they were in the desert.

2. Fire

They needed firewood for cooking the food. This took 4,000 tons of wood filling a few more freight trains each a mile long--just for one day. They were in transit 40 years.

3. Water

If they only had enough to drink and wash a few dishes it took 11 million gallons each day. That's enough water to fill a freight train 1,800 miles long.

4. Shelter
Every time they camped at the end of the day, a campground the size of Rhode Island was required, or a total of 750 square miles.

In addition to all of this, remember the awesome experience at the Red Sea. They had to get across in one night. If they went on a narrow path, double file, the line would be 800 miles long and would require 35 days and nights to get through. So, to get over in one night there had to be a space in the Red Sea 3 miles wide so they could walk 5,000 shoulder to shoulder.

Question: Do you think Moses sat down and figured this entire project out before he decided to **trust** God? I think not! Moses believed God. He had faith that God would take care of everything. So should you! God knows you have need of these things and He has already provided them for you, *"According to His riches in glory by Christ Jesus."*

Realize you do not have to worry, fear or be anxious today. Why? **God is limitless**. He has unlimited resources from which to draw, and He will take care of you. No matter where you are in life, God is not limited by your present circumstances. He is God! As you make His Word final authority in every situation, you'll come out victorious... every time.

Expect His Word to Work
The reason many people never walk in God's ultimate provision is because they don't expect it. They wish for it, but they don't expect it. I believe Moses fully expected

God to come through for them everyday. When you begin to EXPECT, **not** WISH, for God's Word to become true in your life, your faith will become empowered and it will move you toward the fulfillment of your expectation.

The reason many people lack expectation is because their trust is in themselves and not God. Moses could have never fed, clothed and cared for this many people in his own ability. Your faith is not based on you. It has nothing to do with you, your righteousness, or your ability. Faith has everything to do with God, His love for you, His promises to you and His Word. When you begin to trust and rely upon Him and His faithfulness to His Word, it is easy to be full of expectation, full of faith and **free from fear.**

In talking with people who have battled with fear, the one question asked is, "How do I get rid of it?" The Bible sums it up in one word...

LOVE!

That's right! Love is the force which flushes out all fear. 1 John 4:16 says, *"God is love, and he who abides in love abides in God, and God in him."* With God in you, how can you fear? God is love! So, with love in you, how can you fear? You can't!

"There is **no fear in love**; but perfect love **casts out fear**..."

• 1 John 4:18

The world says cope with your fears, the Word says cast it out. Fear is not a feeling, fear is a spirit. It must be cast out! God is not the author of fear, the devil is. Paul wrote to Timothy and said, *"God has not given us the* **spirit of fear**..." (2 Timothy 1:7) So, The Word calls fear a spirit and Christ overcame that spirit. You can too! You must rise up and take authority over that spirit, in the name of Jesus.

How do you cast it out?

1 John 4:18 says through, *"perfect love!"*

What is *perfect love*?

It's love without end. It's complete—lacking nothing. That's the definition of perfect: complete, whole and lacking nothing.

Your love does not need to be displayed only to friends or just when you feel like it. That's love with an end. That's not *perfect love*. Perfect love is displayed even to those that have done you wrong. It is not offended. It does not get jealous, but *perfect love* rejoices when others succeed. Perfect love desires only *to see* the best for others and wants only *to do* the best for others. It doesn't seek to be praised. Why? Because it's **perfect love**! It's complete... lacking nothing.

Do you see how when you're walking and operating in perfect love there is no room for fear? There's no fear because you're secure in perfect love.

How do you refuse to fear? Walk in love!

When you surrender to fear you are refusing to love.
When you surrender to love you are refusing to fear.

If you desire to have a successful life then you must refuse to fear. If you don't, it will overtake you and keep you from all God has destined for your life.

At the beginning of this principle I asked you a question: *What would you attempt to do if you knew you couldn't fail?* I want you to know God's Word never fails. When you Launch Out, in love, according to His Word, you will not fail. Love never fails!

If you've been battling with fear, I have some good news for you, the battles over. You've won through Christ! You are more than a conqueror through the anointed love of God! He has given you, *"Power, love and a sound mind."* When you walk in love, you're walking in truth... Living in Success... Free from fear!

God's Love brings freedom and empowers you to:

Think Big...
Dream Big...
Reach the Goal!

You are a success, not in fear, but in love!

Refuse to fear!

Principle 1

BE THE PERSON GOD CREATED YOU TO BE

Principle 2

LOSE YOUR RELIGION

Principle 3

KNOW WHO YOU ARE IN CHRIST

Principle 4

PUT THE WORD INTO EFFECT

Principle 5

IF YOU FAIL, YOU'RE NOT A FAILURE

Principle 6

SET YOUR MIND FOR SUCCESS

Principle 7

GUARD YOUR MOUTH

Principle 8

PRAY THE PROMISE, NOT THE PROBLEM

Principle 9

REFUSE TO FEAR

Principle 10

GIVE BIRTH TO YOUR DREAMS

Principle 10
Give Birth To Your Dreams

A few days ago I called a friend of mine and asked what he was doing; his response was, "Living the Dream."

Are you living the dream? You should be. You were created to. God gives all of us dreams. It's His will that we see those dreams come into existence. It's important to have dreams. *We fail to grow without something to reach for.* Your dream could be anything - from being an actor to a musician, having a worldwide ministry to owning your home, or from personal growth in your walk with God to overcoming bondage in your life.

Dreams are good to have, but **there's a big difference in *having a dream* and *living the dream***. Moses *had* a dream - to enter Canaan. Joseph *lived* the dream - to rise unto a place of authority and bring deliverance to his family. Both dreams were from God, but only one lived his dream.

<u>The Process of a Dream</u>

> Between the dream and the reality there is a process. Between the promise and the possession there is transition.

The way you respond in the process/transition will determine whether or not you *live the dream* or just *have a dream.* Make a quality decision in your heart right now, at the beginning of this principle, to see every God-breathed dream come to pass in your life. Don't settle for having a dream, LIVE the DREAM!

The process of a dream could be compared to the process of a pregnancy. When a person is pregnant with a dream from God, there are four stages that person goes through, each of which is preparation for birth. Let's take a close look at these four stages so we will be prepared when we are faced with them.

1. Conception
2. Pregnancy
3. Temptation
4. Delivery

Conception stage:
The Lord will often place something in your heart, but you just cannot conceive that God could really mean what He is saying. So most of the time you end up rejecting the seed. You must realize that you cannot get pregnant unless you're able to conceive. You must believe a thing is possible, or nothing even begins. You must be able to *conceive* in your thoughts that even though the thing may be impossible with man, nothing is impossible with God!

Every great invention started at the seed stage. The phonograph, the automobile and the computer all started as thoughts in an individual's mind. They simply *believed* it could happen. At that very moment, they were suddenly catapulted into the second stage...

Pregnancy stage:
Just like a seed planted in the womb, it takes months for the baby to form, so it is with many dreams. They begin with seeds that require time for development. There is *much* planning and preparation before the actual birth. I regret to say, with many dreams most people never make it past the pregnancy.

Why?

Because of the third stage:

Temptation stage:
Why do most people never make it to birth? They grow weary, waiting on God, and try to do something to get things started. Remember Abraham. You must be aware that satan will attempt to get you to give birth prematurely. He tries to get you off of God's timing. If he can't do that, then better yet, he would love to see you *abort* that dream. He is a dream thief. He wants you to give up on that dream.

In the seed stage, dreams are only possibilities; they are not things that will positively come to pass. Much of it is up to you and how you handle yourself during the process of the pregnancy.

So, first you must conceive, then go through the pregnancy, and then endure the temptation to give birth prematurely or abort. But wait, we still have one more stage.

Delivery stage:
How do you give birth to all of your dreams?

"For a dream comes with ***much business*** *and* **painful effort.**"

• Ecclesiastes 5:3 (Amp)

The first time I saw that scripture, I didn't like it. But who said giving birth was easy. It's natural; not easy.

Women who have birthed a child know when you go into the delivery room, you're leaning on your spouse and the doctors for help, but all they can do is say, 'alright now push.'

We've all had to come to the place where we felt like we couldn't go on another second. The Lord would say, "Alright, now bear down and push; you're almost there!"

When you are right at the point of giving birth that's when the pain is the greatest. Don't give up! Don't abort the dream! Try one more time. Push one more time.

"Don't grow weary in well doing, for at the proper time you will reap a harvest if you do not give up."

• Galatians 6:9

Give birth to all your dreams!

Four things to do during the process

1. See The Vision

There's power in vision! Often people get caught up in present circumstances, instead of their vision for the future, and become discouraged. Behind most success stories you'll find an underlying principle; VISION!

What sustained Joseph during his years in prison? His dream! What sustained Moses in the wilderness?

"He persevered because he saw him who is invisible."
•Hebrews 11:27

What do you see in your future? *You'll never seize it until you first see it.* I'm not talking about seeing it first in the natural. I mean see it in your spirit. That is what will sustain you through the obstacles. You'll not get caught up looking at the obstacles, but you'll see the opportunities!

> Vision will sustain you when nothing else will

How do I go from vision to reality?

Habakkuk 2:2 says, "**Write the vision** *and make it plain so he may run who reads it."*

If you want to reach every dream and see your visions manifest from the spirit into the natural; then take these three steps:

<u>Write down</u>...
1. Your dream and the reason you want to fulfill it. Make certain that it's from God. Be sure it is in line with His Word.
2. What you're willing to go through to see it come to pass.

3. Every challenge you'll have to overcome in pursuing it.

A written goal/vision/dream prompts vivid imagery of an end result. When you write down your goals/dreams keep them in the positive. It's okay to identify your obstacles, but don't magnify them. Magnify the end result. Magnify The Word!

Also, connect with someone that has a dream like yours. Whatever you make happen for someone else God will make happen for you.

2. Document Victories

The patriarchs in the Old Testament would build memorials (Altars) to God. They would build this as a place of remembrance. This would serve as a landmark for generations to come so they would not forget all God had done for them.

Whenever the children of Israel were faced with an opposition, one of their major setbacks was that they would easily forget all the things God did for them. They forgot how He brought them out of Egypt, parted the Red Sea, fed them every day and led them to the Promised Land. Whenever they were in need, or if ever God didn't answer them the way *they* thought He should, they were easily persuaded to turn to other gods (Give up on their dream.)

There will be times in your life when you will be tempted to feel discouraged, alone or tempted to turn away from your dreams. In those times you need to *remember* all God has done for you. That's why it's important to document victories in your life so you can see, in times of temptation, how good God is. He desires for you to be a success in life. He wants to see you fulfill all of those dreams because He gave them to you. Document your victories (Set up memorials) and never forget God is a good God.

Begin now!

Document three victories God has done in your life! Begin to praise Him for those victories and then move on to praising Him for the victories to come.

1. ____

____

2. ____

____

3. ____

____

3. Never Doubt God

"So we see that they could not enter in because of unbelief."

• Hebrews 3:19

Think about that for just a moment. The children of Israel had a dream to see the good of the land, to taste the best life, and to enjoy all God had promised to give them. Yet, they doubted and that seed of doubt brought a harvest of not seeing and living the dream! *One day of doubt will destroy a lifetime of dreams.* God's greatest pain is to be doubted. God's greatest joy is to be believed. When you have God's Word on a specific matter, believe Him and nobody else. The information you choose to believe will either give you the power to birth your dreams or keep you barren forty years in the desert.

"Surely goodness and mercy shall follow me all the days of my life."

• Psalm 23:6

David didn't say, "Maybe, possibly, or I hope so." He said, "Surely..." With God it's a *sure* thing. You will give birth to your dreams if you'll never doubt God!

4. Learn to Laugh

That's right! Even laughter will help get you through the process of giving birth to your dreams. There are so many terrible things going on in the world today. If Christians don't watch out, we will fall into the same depression that afflicts the world and we will never see our dreams manifest.

Jesus said, *"The thief comes... to steal"* (John 10:10). One of the ways satan tries to pressure you into aborting your dream is to steal your joy! Sure, some problems are serious, but you gain nothing from exaggerating their importance or dwelling on the miserable side of things. Instead, make a decision that no matter what, you will have joy, and then watch the results you get!

"A cheerful heart brings a smile to your face; a sad heart makes it hard to get through the day."

•Proverbs 15:13

A pastor, who was in the process of seeing some long time dreams come into fulfillment, went to the doctor to discover he had incurred cancer in his body. The spirit-filled doctor told the pastor, who had been eaten up with cancer, to go and buy as many funny movies as he could and laugh. Weeks later, because of prayer and the doctor's advice, there were no signs of cancer to be found in him. Nothing helps get you through the rough times like laughter.

"A merry heart doeth good like a medicine."

•Proverbs 17:22

What does medicine do for you? It assists your body in healing. Laughter does this too. It is good *like medicine*. It provides a marvelous resistance against disease in the body, unhappiness in the home and strife in the church. Medical science has defined laughter as "stationary jogging," because the muscles and blood pressure react in such a healthy way during laughter. After laughing, the body benefits from its relaxed state. Now you can't beat that! You can find something to smile about in almost any situation. Just remember who's on your side!

So, the process to giving birth to a dream is:

1. Conception
2. Pregnancy
3. Temptation
4. Delivery

Today, conceive that God desires to do great things in you, for you and through you. He wants you to *live the dream.*

Realize big dreams require time for development (pregnancy). There is *much* planning and preparation before the actual birth.

Don't give into temptation. During the process:

- See the vision
- Document victories
- Never doubt God
- Learn to laugh

Now you are ready to deliver (give birth to) all God has placed inside of your heart.

Dare to...

Terry Tripp Ministries

Taking God's Word To Unlimited Heights

❑ I would like to be on Terry Tripp's mailing list and receive his itinerary, updates, new books, new CDs, etc.

❑ I would like to schedule Terry to speak at our church, Bible College, Conference, Outreach or Corporate Meeting.

❑ I would like to become a part of The Passionate Society. I pledge $____________ a month to help Terry Tripp Ministries carry The Word of faith, hope and love.

❑ I would like more information on recording in Terry Tripp's studio (The Family Room) in Nashville, TN

Please check your desired box/boxes, print your information below, tear the page and mail to:

Terry Tripp Ministries
P.O. Box 899
Gallatin, TN 37066

www.terrytripp.com

Name____

Address______________________________________

City____________________ST________Zip__________

Email____

Information provided is confidential and will not be shared with anyone.

Join a team of elite people who have a passion for:

The Word
We place God's Word as final authority in life. His Word is the cornerstone on which we can build a sure foundation for our life.

Souls
Every *Passionate Society Member* has the joy in knowing they're a part of a team who have joined forces - reaching the lost - healing the broken - giving life to the dying.

Missions
When you're a part of **"The Passionate Society"** you'll be bringing life, love and a future to your sponsored child every month in India.

Advancing the Goodness of God
Through live meetings, books, CDs, DVDs, radio and TV **"The Passionate Society"** endorses and supports the message that God Is Absolutely Good.

For a gift of any amount, you can join, **"The Passionate Society"** and help to fulfill the command of love. *"Go into all the world and preach the gospel - feed the hungry - clothe the naked - and occupy* (advance The Message) *until I return"* (Mark 16:15, Matthew 25:35-40, Luke 19:13).

How will this benefit you?

Being a part of this unique group of people (*The Passionate Society*) will benefit *you* in many ways.

You'll receive:

1. An investment into your future. Every life that is touched and changed by the power of God's Word will be a reward for you for all of eternity. Just like in a war, those who send and support the troops get to share in the same reward as the troops. In ministry, as you support (send) us, you share in all the rewards.

2. A monthly letter from my heart to yours. The things God places upon my heart for you, you'll receive first hand every month.

3. As a member of this special group of people, you'll receive a card that you can put into your billfold, or your purse, that will identify you as a part of an outstanding class of people *"The Passionate Society."* On that card will be a phone number you can call everyday for prayer. We are here for you to see you have peace in every area of your life. Our number one priority at Terry Tripp Ministries is to minister to you and to see you walk victorious in every area of life.

4. I also desire to see you reach your maximum potential in life, that's why I want to invest in you. Every month I'll send you a gift from our ministry (A new book, a new CD, a coffee mug, a pen) that will have engraved, *The Passionate Society*. Every time you see that gift, you'll be reminded you're a part of a group of people that are passionate about The Word - Souls - Missions - and advancing the Goodness of God.

5. Every three months of the year, you'll receive a CD loaded with Praise and Worship and a Message from me to you.

6. We make you a promise to pray for you everyday. We place a high value upon partnership. Our desire is to see your needs met on every level.

Become a part of
The Passionate Society family.

Join today!